All Europe

LASER 558

Hans Knot

All Europe Radio
LASER 558

Hans Knot

Copyright © 2022

First published 2011 in the Netherlands by
Foundation for Media Communication (SMC)
PO Box 53121 1007 RC Amsterdam, The Netherlands

Layout   :   Jana Knot-Dickscheit
Cover Design: Jan van Heeren

Republished 2022 in the UK by
                    World of Radio Ltd, Hull.

ISBN: 978-1-9004-0130-2

To Jana

and Laser Lovers everywhere

Foundation for Media Communication
(Stichting Media Communicatie)

ACKNOWLEDGEMENTS

The photos and illustrations in this book came from the following sources:

Theo Dencker
Chris Edwards
Karel Gerbers
François Lhote
Peter Messingfeld
Rob Olthof
Hans Verbaan
Leen Vingerling
Hugo van Weeringen
Freewave Media Magazine Photo Archive
Music Media International New York
Offshore Echos magazine
France Photo Archive

MV Communicator

CONTENTS

ACKNOWLEDGEMENTS 4

INTRODUCTION 6

1. FROM ENGLAND TO THE USA 7

2. LISTENING ON AN ANCHOR CHAIN.................15

3. THE SECOND PERIOD 19

4. THE FORGOTTEN ROPE 28

5. ANOTHER DINGHY AND MORE 31

6. SUMMER 1984 36

7. A COURT CASE...44

8. COAST TO COAST 51

9. PLAYING WITH JOURNALISTS.......................60

10. ANOTHER YEAR 72

11. WAS FEBRUARY 1985 BETTER?....................81

12. EARLY MARCH ON THE TV 90

13. STILL THERE, BUT ADRIFT.............................97

14. ALMOST A YEAR 'ON AIR' 102

15. NEGATIVE NEWSPAPER SUPPORT 110

16. BEEB AID - NOT LIVE AID..............................118

17. EUROSIEGE '85 127

18. TV CREW ON THE HIGH SEAS........................133

19. DUTCH NAVY TO ASSIST................................140

20. MORE AND MORE REPORTS 149

21. ACCOMPANIED BY A SISTER-SHIP...............164

INTRODUCTION

It was no big surprise when the radio ship MV Ross Revenge arrived in the Thames Estuary and started broadcasting as the new Radio Caroline. It was August 1983 and after 42 months the station was back on the air after stopping transmissions in March 1980 when their ship MV Mi Amigo sank in a heavy storm.

The new sound of Caroline was boring for many avid listeners as too much nonstop music was played. It wasn't the family station we were so fond of. In those days I wrote for Monitor magazine and Freewave. A third person I have to mention is the late Tom de Munck, who also wrote for the Freewave Media Magazine and as John Wendale for the Free Radio Magazine. Along with others we followed the offshore scene for the readers. The three of us worked closely together in the eighties and succeeded in presenting our work not only to the readers of our magazines but also to several newspapers, magazines and radio stations, who were interested in our work.

Just before Radio Caroline restarted, we had already heard rumours that a new radio ship would appear on the horizon, though it wasn't until November that year that we saw in a trade publication 'Radio News' the first printed report. On November 4th, 1983 they said: 'A new pirate ship is leaving Fort Lauderdale, Florida, today to anchor alongside Radio Caroline off the British Coast. The station, which will be called Laser 730, is expected to arrive off Kent in two weeks. Laser 730 is American-backed and will feature only American personalities, keen to make impression on the European Market. Its music will be Contemporary Hit Radio or Top 40, which has taken many major stateside markets by storm. The mast is 354 feet high and Laser 730 is hoping to achieve a power of 100 kW."

After more than a quarter of a century, I dived into our archives to edit this book 'All Europe Radio, Laser 558'. I hope it will bring back a lot of memories to you, with the happenings of a wonderful radio station from more than 25 years ago, 'All Europe Radio Laser 558'.

Hans Knot,
Gronigen, Netherlands.
November 2011.

CHAPTER 1

FROM ENGLAND TO THE USA

It was on Saturday 27th August 1983, at 15.50 BST, that the former survey ship Gardline Seeker, departed from Lowestoft to sail to the USA. She didn't stop anywhere on the way and arrived in the Tracor Marine shipyard in Port Everglades, Florida, on Wednesday, 28th September. For the time being, it was kept secret that the ship would become a radio transmission vessel.

The first week, until October 3rd, she was in drydock and then she moved to another part of the yard, 'as far away as possible from the prying eyes of news people.' The Communicator was 57 metres long a weighed 489 tons.

On November 17th the ship left Florida and the same day Radio Netherlands brought the news in their media program 'Media Network' with details about the forthcoming radio project:

"In about a month's time Radio Caroline could be joined by a second radio ship anchored in the Thames Estuary and broadcasting on Medium Wave. Sources on board the vessel say it's carrying two 25 kW transmitters and will choose a frequency between 500 and 700 kHz. Interesting is that the ship does not have a regular-style antenna mast; instead, it will hold the antenna aloft using helium filled balloons."

It was also mentioned that the owners would not see the forthcoming station as a 'pirate station'. A group of lawyers had been at work determining that the operation would be perfectly legal and the vessel would have a crew of entirely American citizens. The programming was said to be a lot of music, less talk and even less news. The 'Media Network' show on Radio Nederland announced that: 'Media Management International Incorporated is the owner', a company that had earlier denied any connection to the new project.

After leaving Fort Lauderdale, the ship called in at Sao Miguel Island on November 30th, 1983 in the Azores, where she stayed a few days. Four days later she headed north, to New Ross, in Ireland.

The Communicator arrived on December 8th,1983after a pretty rough voyage. Some of the staff sailed over with the ship, including Commander Buzz Cody, Mighty Joe Young, Jessie Brandon, Melinda Clare, Steve Masters, David Lee Stone, Ric Harris and Blake Williams. During the trip, the DJs kept their spirits up by training in the ship's studios. They used the Audio Technica 1220 recorder and a twelve channel mixing console to make promotion spots for the new station.

The Communicator had fully passed all the tests necessary to obtain a full certificate of seaworthiness. The fire-fighting system alone had cost 11,000 dollars. After the news was spreading around that the ship was anchored in New Ross the owners decided to send her out to sea for a few days so the news people, who were searching for the Communicator, didn't find the ship there between December 12th and 16th 1983. Journalists from around Europe tried to track down the ship and started telling each other the strangest things about her work which led to humorous newspaper articles. For example, The Express newspaper in Munster, Ireland, mentioned on December 16th that the American-owned communicating vessel contained millions of pounds worth of the most advanced satellite linked computer equipment:

"The ship has a Comsat terminal near her stern and by using the Inmarsat satellites, which are 22,500 miles up in space, the crew can be in constant contact with their home base, other ships or any place else in the world. It is possible that the ship could use the NASA Landsat 4 Satellite. This facility is 500 miles up in space and used to be called the Earth Resource Satellite System, which is mainly used by the Navy and the Military. Using that particular system, the ship could accurately pinpoint its position to a matter of yards.'

On the same day NOS radio contacted me for an interview about the new project and so I did some extra research to bring information which wasn't heard before. The interview was in the daily program 'Met het oog op morgen' (With the eye aimed at tomorrow) and the interviewer warned the listeners it might be possible that Radio One, which aired that daily program, could have a lesser audience in the future as a new radio ship was heading for anchorage near the Ross Revenge of Radio Caroline.

New facts I could tell was that the ship was built in 1954 in Lemwerder, Germany and was now owned by the Deka Overseas Corp. On the ship were two 25 kilowatt transmitters, which could be combined, from CSI's Florida factory. On board was an 8 cylinder generator and the price paid for the ship was 65,000 Pounds.

I heard from my contact person in the USA that the ship would leave the harbour in New Ross, Ireland soon and would make its way to the anchorage in the Thames Estuary. Roy Lindau's name was mentioned for the first time when I was asked if the station would carry commercials in their programs. I was able to report that the Laser sales organisation had as a boss, a former vice President of Major Market Radio Sales. I also reported that the ship had on board enough supplies, to last for the next six months.

December 17th,1983 goes into the books as the day that the very first test took place, when the Communicator was still in New Ross. This happened in the very early hours, of course without the use of the balloon. A t-wire was slung between the ships two 40 feet high mast and used as an aerial. To be exactly the test started at 2.50, just for a few minutes and consisted of a blank carrier and a few tuning tones.

A few days later, on December 20th, the MV Communicator left New Ross harbour to arrive on December 22nd in the Thames Estuary. Firstly, she anchored in the 'Quarantine Berth', just off the Kent coast near Margate. The engines were running all the time at 200 rpm just to stay in one place in some of the worst gales of winter. It must have been a bad day for those onboard who had sailed over from Florida.

BBC East TV brought news on the 23rd that the ship was then off the East coast and would be broadcasting soon. On the December 29th, 1983 the Communicator left the berth and sailed north to circle the Ross Revenge, while establishing her position. At 16.00 GMT she dropped her anchor, 2.5 miles south of the Ross Revenge from Radio Caroline.

In the East Anglian Daily Times, an article was published on December 30th headed: 'Warning shot fired by BBC at new pirate'. A new pirate radio station off the East Anglian Coast has received a hostile reception from the BBC. But is has been welcomed by its rival Radio Caroline, broadcasting 14 miles off Walton-on-the- Naze. The new station, Radio Laser, has been given a warning by the BBC because of plans to launch its broadcasts on a frequency close to

Radio Four. There are fears that the station, which is backed to the tune of millions of dollars by a consortium of Americans, may cause disruption to the reception of Radio Four.

A BBC spokesman said it would be a mistake for Radio Laser to stay broadcasting too close to Radio Four's frequency: "It would do neither of us any good. Both stations could suffer from interference. We don't know what will happen as they have not yet started broadcasting. We shall be monitoring the situation and will complain strongly to the Department of Trade if there are problems." A spokesman for the Department said it would seek to prosecute people connected with the new station. There was nothing they could do against the ship itself, the Gardline Seeker, if it kept outside British waters. But it could act against personnel, who came ashore or people who took supplies to the ship, which will be anchored near Radio Caroline.'

A spokeswoman at Caroline's Los Angeles base said that they welcomed the new station: "Competition is good in radio", she said. However, the two stations were aiming for different markets. Caroline specialises in album tracks while Laser will be playing the Top 50 singles. She denied Caroline was facing severe financial difficulties. She also denied rumours that the backers of Radio Laser had withdrawn its financial support of Caroline to back a new project.

We had to wait for some weeks before we heard some news again as on January 19th, 1984, was the big day and at the same time a disaster. The earlier mentioned balloon, a TRF (Tethered Rigid Fin) Model 3500, coloured silver with red fins, was inflated and launched. Next the transmitter was switched on and nothing was heard.

The antenna wire went all the way, virtually to the balloon itself. There were just 12 feet of Kevlar rope, a kind of nylon rope, between the balloon and the top of the antenna. One of the crewmembers told us later: "At the end of the antenna there was very high voltage and this ionized the air around the Kevlar and caused the rope to melt. The balloon just disappeared on its own in a northerly wind, which caused the balloon to drift to France."

Luckily, there was a reserve balloon on board and a two days later this was raised to a height of 350 feet and the transmitter was switched on again. This time was more successful as the signal was heard clearly from the Shetland Islands in the north to France in the south, Germany in the east and Eire in the west.

The station, called itself Laser 730 and used the frequency of 729 kHz. The first carrier was heard at 9.42 GMT on Saturday the 21st of January 1984. At 10.15 GMT the very first record was played on the station, being 'Back in the USSR' from the Beatles and from then onwards we could hear nonstop Beatles music up till the early hours of the Sunday morning.

Helium tanks on deck to fill the balloons

Once again disaster came when also due the bad weather conditions the second balloon got lost. The balloon's suppliers, Haven Industries in Sioux Falls, South Dakota, told us that the balloons were priced at 11,000 dollars each but that the balloons were only guaranteed to withstand 40 MPH winds.

Tom de Munck called me from Zoetermeer, near The Hague, with the news that the new station was on the air. In the western parts of the Netherlands, the signal was receivable. At my place, which is in Groningen in the northern parts of Holland, I tried several receivers and connected them with some cable to my central heating. All for nothing as I did not get the signal out of my radio sets. Silence followed on '730'. Conditions, however, were better in places further away to the East.

In Germany it was Martin van der Ven, well known from his offshore-radio.de internet site, who listened to the nonstop Beatles tests: 'It was around New Year that I first heard of the plans for a new radio station from a ship, coming from the USA. On January 21st , together with my son David, I drove from Munster to my wife's parents in the town of Meppen. It was a cold day and snow was expected. During the car trip I decided once again to search the AM band and at 729 kHz I found a station unknown to me, playing non-stop Beatles music. It was well produced and the signal was really good. Later, I read in a magazine that the signal came from the radio ship MV Communicator.'

The *Media Network* team from Radio Netherlands told their listeners on January 26th, 1984 that the tests had begun and that no spoken identification was heard at all, but a sound effect similar to that used in science fiction films such as Star Wars was heard in between records. Also, some doubt was spoken about the fact the station used the '730': 'If the transmitter should radiate any spurious transmissions on either side of the frequency of 729 kHz, and that harmonics it would cause interference to BBC Radio London on 1458 kHz.

On February 6th, 1984, the TV South local news magazine 'Coast to coast', showed the Communicator in a short feature, bringing the first shots of the ship. The same day we had contact with the office in New York and were told that in about ten days the station would be on the air again. Also was mentioned that the loss of two balloons gave them a lot to think about and it had been decided to build a normal antenna mast on the Communicator.

The lady at the office also mentioned that a special meeting was to be held in London by the financial backers behind the project as well as people from Music Media International and that technicians on the Communicator were working very hard to get the station on the air before the day of that meeting. Six days later, on February 12th at 11.30 that Sunday morning, a signal appeared again on 729 kHz. It was very rough sounding and for the first hour you could hear the transmitter regularly being switched on and off. This went on to 13.17 GMT when the high voltage flying around in the unmatched temporary wire aerial caused some capacitors to blow up in a loading coil assembly, and the station was again off the air. The following day, a very low power test was held using an aerial hanging between the two ship masts. Robin Banks, formerly with Caroline and RNI in the seventies, was responsible for the temporary technical outfit.

We had to wait until February 14th when, at 13.23 the first voice was heard on the station. It was American Blake Williams telling us it was a test broadcast on 729 kHz from the MV Communicator. Also, announcements were made in English, German and Dutch by engineer Paul Alexander Rusling. The ship's location was given out, and so was the address for reception reports being MMI, 341 Madison Avenue, New York, N.Y. 10017 in the USA. The tests went on for five days, initially with recorded promos between the music but soon the two technicians and a then Johnny started to present programs. Good old Johnny Lewis was the first British DJ to host a programme on the new offshore radio station. He only mentioned his first name but when he gave best wishes to Marc Jacobs in Groningen, we knew for sure it was him.

I know now that he had arrived in Whitstable with John Burch to visit their friend Paul Rusling, who was secretly handling UK logistics for the station's owner. Since losing the balloons, the American crew wanted to leave the ship and Paul urgently needed replacements, who could help to try and get the station operational.. Johnny had an overnight bag with him and was willing to sail out to sea immediately. Paul took out Johnny, another offshore radio engineer, Robin Banks and a new captain and brought off eleven of the American crew.

The two CSI transmitters and combiner

After a few days, the nonstop Beatles music was supplemented by Rolling Stones tracks and then a short time later by other rock music. All the music was played in from NAB tape cartridges. The studios were equipped with Broadcast Electronic Model 3000 'triple-stack' cart' machines. Only once during the tests was the name 'Laser' heard: 'Time on Laser is two minutes past one. Oh! I shouldn't have said that!'

The music was being played in from the 1800 NAB cartridges in the studios, which were being filled with songs transferred from vinyl. Ric Harris, who became a deejay on Laser 558 remembers: 'Most CHR stations go with about 250 records but on Laser we had more, perhaps 900 to 1200 because of the 'longer daily listening' time a European audience give to radio. In any event, the cartridge count was about 1800. We bought them in kit form and loaded the tape into them ourselves to match the song lengths'.

By the weekend it was decided that a better aerial system was going to be erected on board and Johnny Lewis and Blake Williams ended the last in the first series of test transmissions. They told the listeners that they hoped to be back in ten days or at least a few weeks with a new aerial system as well as a stronger signal. They said that the frequency would be probably change, but they should stay tuned to that end of the Medium Wave, for the new sound of Laser Radio.

On February 17th we learned from the New York office that a new mast was on the way to the ship, which would be 210 feet high They promised also that very soon a postal address in Waterford, Ireland, would be used on the air, which also never became reality.

The tests on 729 kHz went on for several more days and on March 4th the very last test on 729 kHz could be heard with programs presented by Blake Williams and Johnny Lewis. The test ended as sometimes, sparks to the deck. Blake Williams promised at the end of test programming: "We will be back in ten days up to three weeks and it will blow your mind."

At the end of the first period of test programs, news came in from a listener in Froland, Norway. Dag Aanonsen wrote that the Communicator was formerly owned by Stavangerske Dampskipelskap' and that the ship, then name MV Tananger, passed his shoreline a few times a week for many years as it was used to carry goods and a few people between Oslo and Bergen.

Chapter 2

LISTENING ON AN ANCHOR CHAIN

Looking back into the history on Offshore Radio we will find hundreds, maybe thousands of people who have worked for one of the many radio stations which brought their sounds through the medium wave into the many households all over Western Europe. Some of them spent a few years or more on the same station, others left after one stint as seasickness made it impossible to life a normal life on a radio ship, as long as we could speak about 'a normal live'. But there's another group of people working from international waters which we shouldn't forget. It's our offshore radio hard core. People who are going from one station to another and coming back again and do their utmost to bring the best sounds around. We could mention names like Alan West, Graham Gill and Peter Chicago.

Also, Johnny Lewis, aka Stephen Bishop, aka John Moss, must be mentioned as he worked for several offshore radio stations, including Radio Caroline, Voice of Peace and more. One day early in 1984 he worked in the beautiful country of Ireland, in Waterford to be exactly at ABC Radio. Within a month he got a phone call there with the question if he would like to go back to sea again. The answer was simply one word: 'Yes". Let's follow his memories:

'It was February 4th, 1984 that I went out to the MV Communicator. I remember that it was a very rough day and so we had a fairly long and rough ride out to the ship. When we finally got alongside the ship, the first thing we could see was loads of lights, because they got massive 500 Watt lights on the deck to illuminate the working space. We could see all those helium tanks for the balloons. The ship was quite a way out of the water, so there was a rope ladder to get on the deck, which in that sort of weather is not too good! However, we managed to get on without falling in. At that stage most of the American crew went off, leaving just a few of us: a few American deejays, a new captain, me and Blake Williams were the ones to make the Communicator our home for the next couple of weeks.

"Once we were alone, it was decided to get the station on the air, not using the helium balloon, as that didn't work. Or should I say I worked but not far too long? I think they were designed to work for up to sixty knots on land, and of course on a ship when you get winds of about twenty knots it starts to roll and you're getting then a force of forty knots as the ship is rolling. You only need a force five to get in problems, when you were out there. That's my theory why it didn't work and I don't think a balloon system would work anyway: I'd go for the good old tower system. Anyway, rather to wait for new balloons, it was decided to put a 'T' aerial up."

"Now, for anyone who's technical, trying to make a 'T' resonate is not the easiest job in the world. Basically, what you have to do is to try to get as much copper above the ship as possible. Ideally, you want as much of it in the vertical section. We could only get 45ft vertical which didn't help matters at all. We got to work on this 'T' anyway and I was surprised it worked. We made the 'T' work literally using all the copper, and it was very heavy copper. The top loading section was, I think, ten foot across and sixty foot long, and there were six strands at sixty foot long, all with shorting bars going across with ten foot spacings between them. We hoisted this thing up in the air and my God, did it look ugly when it was up there! So, we went downstairs and fired up the transmitter and it didn't like it all. There were some cracks and some bangs; at this point we decided to put yet another piece of wire on the end of the 'T', running down to the top of the bridge, where we would have this big coil."

"The actual case of the coil was made out of wood, which is not the best thing to use when it gets wet. We didn't know that this wood had already been wet and when we switched the transmitter on, on the Sunday morning, we switched it on gradually at about 500 Watts. And we thought that we had cracked it. When we went up to 1.5 kW, we saw flames everywhere. Of course, we decided that was it and went off the air quickly and no use of that coil could be done in the future. We decided to build another coil and Blake Williams got to work on this one but we hadn't any material to build a coil. Being on a 'pirate radio ship' you had to bodge things, so to make a coil was we got two bits of padding from some tube cartons."

The end padding was two feet square and in it we stuck four fluorescent tubes. We then wound cable round them to make a new coil. We put it on and it worked and unfortunately the transmitter just didn't like it, and we couldn't get any more than 3 kW out of it. At this stage we had, what is called 'downward mod', in other words the negatives were higher than the positives, whereas you want the positive peaks on your modulation higher than your negatives one. So, we thought we'd try another idea and brought the coil down from the top of the bridge and put it above the transmitter so instead having the coil at the end it'd be at the front.

At the same time, we lengthened the aerial slightly by putting two pieces of wire running from the stern mast – insulated of course – right down almost to the little 'lollipop', the Satcom dome at the back, and then again wire running from the forward mast down to the anchor chain. We had wire everywhere on that boat! We had people come alongside when we were on the air and say: 'Can we come on board and have a look? And we said no, not unless you want to be electrocuted!'

Even we had to watch where we walked. On Tuesday afternoon we switched the transmitter on, gradually we turned the power on up to 5 kW, and then we tried it with modulation – and it appeared to have liked it. We were getting 133% positive peaks, 95% negative peaks and that was ideal. Perfect! We'd cracked it as far as the listeners were concerned, but the aerial was sparking everywhere. You normally put what they call corona shields on the end of aerials, or any sharp point of the aerial, so that you don't get sparks flying out anywhere. Because what radio waves don't like is bits on aerials that bend so you put a corona shield on. So, at nights, if you can imagine it, sparks were sparking with the modulation peaks; whenever we played 'Under cover of the night' by the Rolling Stones, which starts with a very hefty drum-beat, it was amazing to see these sparks shooting out for about two feet! You could actually go to the front of the boat and listen to the station on the anchor chain."

We had a very highly 'Q' on the Communicator. We had to back off the combiner, we took a lot of coils out of the aerial tuning units, and we used one of the coils; the 'Q' on that is ridiculous, you only had to move the tap slightly and you lost resonance completely. In half a turn you'd lose it. At first, we tried the old 'on-off', quickly have a look at the meters, you know' because we knew that 5 kW into the dummy load which was a pure 50 ohms was 10 Amps, so that's what we were going on at first. We did do it fairly well; we got it down to about 1 amp.

Our English boss Paul spoke to Ronan on the satellite link and got permission to borrow a piece of kit that he knew Chicago had on the Ross Revenge. A few hours later, there was a knock on the side of the boat. It was Tom Anderson and Bill from the Caroline ship and they said:" We've brought you a present - they'd brought us their aerial bridge, a piece of test kit that can measure aerials. What was going to be a few day's work only took us about half an hour. We were doing it at low power, but had to wear gloves. We eventually got a match anyway. It was very critical; you're talking about of less than half a turn. Quite a lot of trial and error.

If one of those wires, for instance, that one was coming down, coming across from the bridge into the centre feed, just part of its insulation, if it would swing and hit something and the insulator went, which it did a couple of times, we would lose the whole matching. The ammeter would go bananas, I'd got 15, sometimes even 20 Amps just by that little bit going. We kept the test going until the Sunday afternoon, and then decided to call it a day, mostly because the people on the boat were a bit tired because there wasn't too many of us on board. Believe it or not but we got about two thousands letters after those five days of test transmissions, which was not bad at all knowing that we didn't warn anyone that we would go on the air.

People may remember that Blake Williams and I did the last program and we had a lot of fun, we were sounding so jolly in those days. We had fun on the Communicator as well as on the Ross Revenge, where we went out to a lot to have tea and home brew and our friends from across the road came to our ship to have a good shower; it was just like neighbours.

Modulation Monitor and Processing

Chapter 3

THE SECOND PERIOD

Initially, I thought it was an April Fool's Day joke when I heard on the evening of April 1st, 1984 that the Communicator had lost her main anchor chain. It snapped in a storm at 20.45 BST. The vessel's onboard anchor was quickly put down and the drifting was stopped. For the next sixty-one days this spare anchor kept the radio ship secure. Johnny Lewis remembers the night: "All that weekend we had some really bad weather, North East eight and nine and we were clanking on the anchor-chain all Sunday afternoon. At about a quarter to nine, while we were watching 'Spitting Image', there was an almighty clonk.

'Bang' it went, the whole ship shuddered, it came up and it just turned side wards. We all looked at one another and we knew what had happened straight away. But we kept watching the telly. After the program I went out and I think our skipper thought I was going to have a look at the anchor, but I wasn't. I was going downstairs to my cabin to have a listen to some music. In fact, I turned on the radio. I'd got Radio Caroline on and Tom Anderson was on the air and said something about the little red boat, who seemed to be moving about quite a bit.

I was just wondering at that point if that was a hint that we were adrift from them, but I didn't take any notice and just kept listening. I remember at one point looking out of my porthole thinking: 'Oh, it's a clear night, the old Tongue looks nice and clear, and so does Margate.' Just after that our skipper came in the cabin and said: "We appear to be adrift". I thought that would explain why it was so clear.

There was no panic at all, we went all to the bridge to ascertain where we were. Our first thought was to drop the spare anchor but then we checked were we were first, because we didn't want to make the same mistake as was made with the Mi Amigo in 1975. We wanted to know where we were in case of, we dropped the anchor on a sandbank. At that point we were out of the Knock Deep, we'd actually gone right over the Kentish Knock."

"We were still drifting, and we knew then that we were heading to deeper water, so the Skipper went down to try to start the main engine. He was having problems down there with that so he had it to pieces; you've got to give him credit for taking it to pieces in that sort of weather. We were with four on board, next to us there were Malcolm and Blake and they all worked very hard to get the Communicator going and bring it back into calmer waters, after weather became normal again.'

On April 13th an American citizen appeared before Sheerness Magistrates Court as he was connected to Laser, had been caught and had to pay 500 Pounds. The local newspaper 'Sheppey Gazette' brought the first news about the case:

"An international scheme to run a pirate radio station was foiled after a police raid at Chalk Wharf in Queensborough. Appearing in court was a 30 year old American brought over to this country by a highly-organised and well-financed operation aiming to set up a radio station on a ship anchored in international waters. The person, David Irvine, had been hired to eliminate technical difficulties experienced by the station and had designed masts to hold broadcasting equipment."

The masts were being constructed on the wharf in Queenborough and were discovered by Police and an official from the Department of Trade and Industry (DTI) on March 16th, 1984. The defendant was in charge of the project in the UK and had been paid 3,750 dollars by a Panamanian Company. The masts were being welded together and 10,000 Pounds were paid to the contractors for anticipated costs of labour and materials.

Funny to read in the article that the solicitor defending Captain Irving, Gregory Treverton, told the court that Irving was a graduate of the US Coastguard Academy, was a man of good character, who would not have taken on the job had he realised it was against the law. When he came over to England in December 1983, he had been told that there were no illegalities involved, provided the ship remained outside the UK limits. In addition to the 500 Pounds, 30 years old David Irvine also had to pay 50 Pounds in court costs.

Another article in the local 'Thanet Gazette' said that police and customs officials had, since the start of test broadcasts from Laser 730, kept a close watch on ports such as Ramsgate, Margate and Queensborough to prevent anyone supplying the Communicator.

Two other persons, who appeared in court: Clive Ian Payne of Halfway on Sheppey had the charge against him withdrawn and he was allowed to leave the dock. The third one, Nicholas Murray (39) of Minister did not appear. It was mentioned by the defending solicitor, Mr Treverton, that Mr. Irving would return to the USA. Lucky enough for the Laser organisation other builders and welders could be found to build another mast system, this time on board the orange painted radio ship.

On May the 6th the work was ready and a transmitter was switched on for the first time since many weeks. At 12.01 BST an unmodulated carrier was heard for just more than two hours. Was the station ready to start full broadcasts? May the 7th the transmitter was put on at 7.16 BST and brought a carrier only, which lasted to 10.45 BST. An hour of non-stop music followed, the first record being 'Radio Ga Ga' by Queen. This was followed by more tuning tests which lasted up till the following night when at 01.05 BST the transmitter went off the air. Long days would start for the Monitor and Freewave listening team. The next day tests were heard between 7.04 and 16.02 BST.

Nothing more was heard on the frequency until the early morning of May 16th when we switched on around 6.30 in the morning. The signal received came, at irregular times, clearly into our house in Groningen, which is near to the German border in the North of the Netherlands. For more than three days, the nonstop music was on, interrupted for a few minutes from time to time. On the 19th of May the transmitter was off between proximally 06.00 in the morning and 5.30 in the afternoon. Also, the days following brought at several times nonstop music on 558 kHz. We learnt from our contacts that the first period of tests on this frequency were held with a maximum power of 3kW and during the period power was added to a maximum of 16kW.

The same day we had a call with the New York office and spoke to Roy Lindau who told us that there were some hot news items to be mentioned. The first one was that former investors, organised within DEKA Overseas, would step backwards and that new investors had signed contracts worth 1,5 million dollars and would work under the name 'Eurad SA'. Lindau mentioned that the investors put the money on the table, although no advertisers at all were booked for the station: "We won't give any advertiser a chance to book airtime before we have built a big audience. In the future we hope to book multinational advertisers and hope to give them not only a big audience but also a formula which cannot be neglected."

In the meantime, rumours went around that some of the ILR stations were very unhappy with the forthcoming start of the new station. Cecilia Garnett, the Managing Director of Kent's ILR station Invicta Sound and Eddie Blackwell, former offshore radio station Radio London sales manager in the sixties of last century and in 1984 the MD of Radio Essex, took every possibility to say that the government had to stop all the offshore radio stations, as they were a threat for the Independent Local Radio stations. Asking Lindau for a comment he told us: "They don't understand that probably the listener will choose our station above those organised by the government rules. It is very healthy to be competitive and it will give them something to think about how they organised themselves."

In the days before the station officially started, I brought one of my tape recorders and transistor radios to my office at the University. All programming could be recorded reel to reel, either at home or at the University. Strange enough the quality of the signal in the centre of our town had not too much influence by the many strip lightning in the several offices surrounding us. I was ready for it and had bought many tapes so I could record as much as possible from the new station, which sounded in my ears as they would be bringing back the good old days of Radio London and Swinging Radio England from the sixties.

Officially it was planned to start programming on Monday May 21st, which was a Bank Holiday in England. But the modulation was not good at all, so they decided to solve the problem and start some days later. In the meantime, we were told by Roy Lindau that a month after the official start a listener's research would be done to find out how many of the 190 million European would tune in to the new Laser 558.

It was on Thursday May 24th that I started recording at 07.00 CET, as it turned out the station was already on the air with presented programs. No announcement had been made that programs should be a regular from that day on, so I presume not many listeners have tuned in to that very first hour, presented by Ric Harris. Years later, a recording of the opening turned up I can tell how it sounded. First some spoken jingles in several languages for Laser 558, this on the sound of waves of the sea, followed by an official opening.

'Good morning I'm Rick Harris and on behalf of David Lee Stone, Jessie Brandon, Steve Masters, Jerry Young, Tim Levansaler, Bill Voigt, Dennis Lassier, David London, Michael Wilson and four dozen other people I'm pleased to introduce you to a brand new radio station All Europe Radio, Laser 558.Broadcasting live from international waters from the MV Communicator we promise to bring you 54 minutes of international hit songs each hour we broadcast, all hits all the time. Plus, we keep you informed with the news of the world hourly. And speaking for all of us, welcome to Laser 558, where you're never more than a minute away from music, starting now!'

Jessie Brandon, Ric Harris, Paul Dean,
Steve Masters and David Lee Stone

Returning to the diary I can mention that during the first days the station was on the air for 20 hours a day and those hours were shared by four deejays: Ric Harris, David Lee Stone, Jessie Brandon and Steve Masters; each doing five hours shows. Also, news was read by one of them. Two names missing from the earlier lineup of American deejays: Buzz Cody and Melinda Clare, who were so fed up with waiting for the station to start that they both headed home to the USA. Another person, not yet mentioned, was Mighty Joe Young. He would later present programs but was mainly on the Communicator for doing engineering work.

Let's go back to the memories from Martin van der Ven in Germany: 'After hearing the nonstop Beatles music test in January I was very sharp to hear more and tuned into the used frequency on regular base. I had to wait till May 24th hearing the first sounds from Laser 558 with Ric Harris in the morning, just before driving to work. A pity that reception was not too good, which was due to the interference caused by the Deutschlandfunk, on 548 kHz. However, reception of the Laser signal in Millingen, at my parent's house, was far much better and so some days later I made my very first Laser recording, which much more to come. I enjoyed the programs but too less information was given in those days about the work and living on the ship, as we were used to with other stations from international waters.'

It would take two days before we heard another new voice, which would be a regularly one. It was Paul Dean, reading the news at 11.00 BST and at 14.00 he was doing a radio show for four hours and with him arriving and no one leaving all programs were shortened four hours. Paul Dean was, for those who listened in the early seventies to RNI, a familiar voice as he worked there for some time as 'Paul May'. Then it became Sunday and, to our surprise, the Sundays became known as 'Sixties Sunday' on Laser 558, meaning that the station played only oldies from that period.

On Wednesday 28th I had some contacts with people in the east of England as well in the west of the Netherlands and they told me that the signal came in very clear in those parts of their countries. In London the signal was better than the one from Caroline, which was hardly receivable in some of the Greater London areas.

On the 29th of May, the newspaper 'Haagsche Post' reported in a short message that probably Laser would get a sister station on the MV Communicator and the name 'Radio Maeve' was mentioned. It would be a Belgian organisation, which had planned to buy airtime. It was just another of the many rumours which were connected to Offshore Radio. The organisation Radio Maeva had nothing to do with the rumours, which had been first mentioned on May 8th in the

Daily 'Volkskrant'. Probably without checking, the journalist from 'the Haagsche Post' had just believed that the information was true.

When I opened my long-running PO Box 102 in Groningen on Tuesday 29th of May, I was surprised to find a big yellow envelope, sent out from the New York offices from Music Media International. In the envelope a press report, photographs as well as a sample of the blue and gold logo, as used on the t-shirts, and other promotional material.

The MMI press report started: "The launch of Laser 558 All Europe Radio earlier this week brings another Pan European broadcast medium within reach of multi-national companies with global brand strategies. American deejays are playing hit music to listeners in nine countries from aboard a radio ship in the North Sea, making it possible for world brands to talk to. Pan European advertising had been a hot concept in advertisement circles lately, but there's been much more talk than action,' says Roy Lindau, President of Music Media International, Inc., the exclusive worldwide representative of the station. Heavy governmental control of media has made it difficult to advertise from nation to nation or even city to city! Until now the concept has stymied by a lack of advertiser supported media with significant penetration of European households."

In 1983 Ted Levitt at Harvard University wrote an article about the global corporation which operates as if the entire world or major regions of it were a single largely identical entity: 'more and more companies are trying to develop markets by appealing more to what people have in common than to what makes them different. Roy Lindau said: 'That's just the way we're doing at Laser 558 All Europe Radio. Pop music is just one thing most young Europeans 15 to 34 have in common, and Laser 558 is giving them more than they can get elsewhere.' By reading this statement in the press report, I remember that I felt very lucky as I was at that stage belonging to the target group, as I was in May 1984 34 years of age!

Another person already on the Communicator also was mentioned in the report. David Lee Stone, one of the DJs who was also station manager: "We play records from all the charts over Europe. Most European hits are in English, so it's the primary language of the station, but you'll hear occasionally records, promotions and commercial spots in other languages. We want to be perceived to be a true Pan European station. Over 164 million listeners in nine countries are in our reception area and we want to attract as many listeners as we can."

The press report also mentioned that a commercial booked through the MMI office in New York, by their computer, could be aired the same day on '558'. The rates for airtime ranged from 40 dollar to 250 dollars for a thirty second spot, depending what time of day it was transmitted. Spots could be recorded on forehand and delivered by the advertiser, recorded by the station, read out live by the deejays (even bilingual was an option) and in sponsored special programs. Lengths were between 15 and 60 seconds and when one was being aired, no announcement was made by the DJ. The station repeatedly stated on the air that: 'You're never more than a minute away from music.'

Reading again the press report after almost 26 years it gave me a big smile to see which advertisers were promised by Lindau and his staff: 'Goodyear, Levis, Pepsi, Coke, Kelloggs, Mars, Kodak, Polaroid, Pampers and Gillette are just a few of the world brands active throughout Europe who are prospects for the new Pan European electronic media like Laser 558. We'll be offering them the opportunity for testing and learning at very low costs.' By the way, during the first week of official programming from All Europe Radio Laser 558 no commercial was played on the air but would soon follow.

It was May 30th that Laser advertised their promotional material as the first commercials. The Laser t-shirts were first, with logo I mentioned earlier. It was very nice to see that Jessie Brandon was wearing the same t-shirt at the Laser Reunion in November 2009. She has a very good heart for memories too.

Weeks before the Annual Radio Day in Amsterdam, in 2009, Jessie sent me some posters, including the wall poster with the DJ team showing some of those who were never heard on the station. It was the same wall poster which was on the air as a 'in-house commercial' on Laser 558.

The first day of June another commercial was played, again a promotional one for the Laser Souvenir edition, which showed the fitting out of the radio ship in Florida as well as presenting the deejay team. Badges for Laser followed eight days later, carrying the earlier mentioned logo. A nautical showing a blue and gold rectangle (although to my eyes it was more yellow). This logo meant in international code: 'I want to communicate with you.'

Of course, there were also the commercials on the air asking the listener to become a member of the Laser Club. A Laser club card, stickers, photographs were sent to members who had paid to the MMI address at Madison Square Garden in New York.

Several times a day, a winning club number would be read out by the DJs and they would receive some surprises. I got of course the press reports but never sent money to New York for a membership. But, to my surprise, I got the club member package and some days later my name and number was read out on Laser 558. I was winner of the surprise bag, which came a few weeks later:

More promotional material followed from Laser including two LP's: The Communards first and then one from Boy George. At the end of May, a new address was heard on the station, used for requests and dedications: "Write to whichever disc jockey you wish, care of: MV Communicator, PO Box 1892, Grand Central Station, New York, 10163, U.S.A.

The Communicator's third studio – Laser's newsroom

with a KayPro 4 computer – the first in offshore radio.

Chapter 4

THE FORGOTTEN ROPE

Think about the idea that you've volunteered and later worked as a paid deejay on a radio station in a minor radio market in the USA and you want to spread your wings to something bigger. You've looked several times in the trade magazine, looking for a job which could be better than you have at the moment. Suddenly one day you see an advertisement whereby deejays are asked to work together in an international radio project called 'All Europe Radio Laser 558'. This could be the dream for making the big career step you wanted. So, making a demo and writing a letter to the Music Media International (in this case) was the next to do. Within days you're informed that broadcasts will be from international waters in the North Sea and it will be a good paid job, with free accommodation, food, drinks and, if wanted, cigarettes too.

The chance of a lifetime and suddenly some weeks later you find yourself back in an inflatable boat. It happened to four crewmembers of the MV Communicator on June 1st, 1984, including DJs Paul Dean and Ric Harris. Next to them were Captain Tim and deckhand Chico.

The first intimation to the listeners that something was amiss came at about 20.30 BST when Jessie Brandon made a remark, on Laser 558, to the effect that they had lost their captain in the inflatable boat and if anyone could find him would they please send him home! No further references were made until the 22.00 news headlines when the last item to be read out was: "Ross Revenge, if you're there, give us a call, will you on channel seventy-seven." Following that, a message was repeated a few times in the next twenty minutes by a very concerned deejay Steve Masters. But, although the message was meant to those on board the Radio Caroline ship; more people listened in, including the coastguard.

What would happen if they were picked up using the help of the authorities? Would they be arrested, taken to court, punished and even deported? As they had American passports, they could be breaking Immigration laws, though not the Marine Offences Bill of 1967. Bringing the four into England was not a good move in the first weeks of the new All Europe Radio ~ Laser 558.

The drama shifted to the maritime VHF band where shortly after 23.30 BST North Foreland Radio brought the following message: "Inflatable dinghy with four persons on board. Engine failure near radio ship Communicator'. Next the position of the radio ship was given and the statement that the lifeboat from Ramsgate was launched and was in proceeding. Everyone in that part of the Thames Estuary was asked to look out for the four: "Ships with information please inform to North Foreland Radio."

The next relevant information came from one of the many ships, the car-ferry Olau Britannia, which was responsible for the ferry line between Flushing in the Netherlands and the harbour of Sheerness. From the bridge of the Olau Britannia the message was reported that there was a faint echo on their radar, bearing 035; 7.7 miles from the Tongue Light Vessel. The following update from Thames Coastguard came in just after midnight: "Information is requested of inflatable dinghy with four persons aboard. Engine failure near the radio ship Communicator at 20.15 GMT in position 51.38 North and 01.33 East. Fishing vessel 'Tarka' in area and searching."

Thames Coastguard, from that stage on, coordinated the search and mentioned that searching next to the Ramsgate lifeboat was Rescue helicopter 66. Some minutes later, the good news was released, as just after midnight it was heard that the four had been rescued and taken aboard on the FV Tarka. Thames Coastguard then asked the crew on the fishing vessel what they wanted to do with the rescued crew. The answer was to return them to the radio ship'. No comment was given on the answer and Thames Coastguard sent out one final message about this case: 'Cancel 'PAN' broadcast. Inflatable and four occupants are safe on fishing vessel Tarka. All well."

What had happened earlier that day during the David Lee Stone program? He had informed the listeners that the ship was moving under her own power, i.e., the engines were running at that moment. They were on their way to a new mooring with a speed of about 2 knots. They arrived and dropped the anchor at their new position. It seems they were not sure enough if the anchor came down correctly so Captain Tim decided to make a closer inspection. The four afore-mentioned crew climbed into the inflatable dinghy to examine the anchor chain. But they forgot something very important - to connect a rope between the dinghy and the radio ship.

Just after 0.30 BST on June 2nd the good news had arrived on Laser 558 as Steve Masters played James Taylor's 'You've got a friend' and dedicated it: "For friends that help friends. And thanks a lot to the fishing boat Tarka for helping ours, OK? Hope you have a big catch all of your years."

After receiving two small remarks that, in reality, the happenings were just a bit more than was mentioned on the radio, Jesse Brandon came back to me with her story: 'The guys in the inflatable boat had been to visit the crew from Radio Caroline on their ship MV Ross Revenge. As both our managements had ordered us to have no contact, it was hard to mention the real reason on the air. There was our 'illegal contact' and they were all passed out having been drinking heavily. Just as our guys would have been if they'd been on their own ship instead of trying to get back to it!

We watched them approach from the poop deck and then drift further away and soon realised that they weren't clowning around anymore, Paul Dean had been dipping Ric's head over the side into the water and laughing and they were waving a liquor bottle, I told the others. Realising that there was nothing we could do, I woke up Bill Voigt, the ship's Chief Engineer. He was furious! With Tim off the boat, Bill was now acting captain as the senior seaman. Tim should have told him that he was leaving and Bill was now on duty and ought to have been up. That was when Bill got on the radio telephone. We were told later that the Royal Yacht Britannia had also responded to the call, offering to divert 'with her own passengers aboard' to assist in the search.'

That evening, those on the Communicator were happy, as were the listeners who had followed the messages during the program that evening and into the night. Maybe the crew on the fishing vessel 'Tarka' had one drink that night to celebrate saving some people in a dinghy. Memories from more than 25 years ago; a nice surprise to get some memories from former Laser crew to verify the story.

In June 1984, Roy Lindau was interviewed by Anglia Television: "We have all Americans aboard, they all have American passports, and we're owned by a non-European company. As long as we remain like that, we're totally legal. The sea is free!' In the many months to come, he would find out the British authorities had other ideas about 'freedom'.

Chapter 5

ANOTHER DINGHY AND MORE

Sometimes we thought Laser could be a bit more professional. For instance, we heard on June 6th, Steve Masters announcing four times that the news would be on at 10 o'clock, but nothing happened. No reason was ever given why it was not on.

A few days later, the 10th, Steve Masters introduced a competitor to the famous Caroline bell by playing the sound of a bell when he was making a time check. It seemed to us he was not one of the best deejays Laser had. He played four artists twice in one show, which isn't a good programming tactic. But he would not last too long on Laser 558 as he was the first deejay who left the station within a month after the first official program on the air. On June 16th Steve Masters started his last show at 21.00 BST to go into a new day and closed for the last time his program on Laser 558 at 01.00 BST on June 17th. He left the station to seek a living in Paris, France). On the 17th of June Laser had its first breakdown when the station suddenly closed down at 11.15 during the David Lee Stone program. It would take some days before Laser returned.

Reason enough to get in contact with Roy Lindau and he promised that problems would be solved. He told us that Mighty Joe Young, the official program director, was ill but hopefully would rejoin the team soon. He also mentioned that in the New York office an official request from the Irish Public Broadcaster RTE asking that Laser change frequency or lower their power as there was too much interference with one of their transmitters in Ireland. Lindau was very enthusiastic on the enormous number of letters that came into the New York Office on a daily basis. He was very proud that one of the letters came from Paul and Linda McCartney, wishing the station a lot of luck and confirming that they liked it a lot.

In the early hours of June 22nd Laser 558 was back on the air. At 05.00 normal programming resumed and that very day brought us two new presenters being Tommy Rivers and another lady, Holly Michaels. June 28th the British Channel Four had a short item in which they asked people in the street if they ever heard about Laser.

It was good to see that all did know about the station and gave very positive feedback on the questions.

On June 30th another new DJ, who would become one of the big ones on the station, was first heard between 17.00 and 21.00 hours being Charlie Wolf. Around 22.39 Laser was off the air due to generator problems and the next morning, during the Ric Harris Breakfast show, it was technician Chico who told how he solved the problems. He was the only not American onboard the Communicator at that time and originated from Cuba and was very well loved due his technical knowledge.

Charlie Wolf

Early June I had another phone call with Roy Lindau and he told us that they'd organised a special research to learn more about the knowledge of the English language in their reception area. From this they learned that in the Netherlands 67% of the people spoke English fluently. It was decided to produce some Dutch language jingles and to play more golden oldies in the future, which were produced in the sixties by Dutch Beat Groups.

July 5th was also a remarkable day as it was the very first day the DJs spoke about the content of the first letters, they had just received from the New York office. Almost six weeks after the station came on the air and I presume they didn't use 'Priority Airfreight' to get the letters to the Communicator.

July 8th saw some changes and it brought Holly Michaels onto the chair at 17.00 then Charlie at 21.00 until close down time.

Some in British Governmental circles were probably astonished to read the news in the London Evening Standard on July 9th, 1984. Tony Blackburn, the then 40 year old BBC Radio London presenter, who became famous on Radio London as well as on Radio Caroline, told how he was planning to horrify his BBC bosses by hiring a pirate radio deejay to stand in for him, later that month, on his BBC Radio London morning show: 'Blackburn has taken the extraordinary step of contacting Laser 558. He has asked Jessie Brandon, an American presenter, to fill in for him on his BBC Radio London program. Blackburn has no qualm about singing the praises of Laser, which has been steadily pinching listeners from Radio One for the past six weeks.'

Tony Blackburn said: "Laser is a brilliant station, much more fun than other pop stations I won't name. I hope its presence will give the legal pop stations the kick up the bum they deserve. Jessie is the best girl disc jockey around at the moment and she's the ideal person to fill in for me while I'm away."

July 15th, we heard the very first announcement for the Laser Lover Communicator Road Show and the DJ mentioned was Robbie Day. He was also active for the Caroline Road Show in 1979 and 1980. Charlie Wolfe said that he had never heard of Robbie Day and wished the visitors for the road show good luck. That day also brought the start of the Concert Agenda, which became a regular feature on Laser 558, which was read from the Musical Express. Holiday time in July and so we didn't listen a lot but July 22nd brought us Paul Dean back on the air, shifted between 05.00 and 09.00 in the morning and from that day on, talking about holidays, the listeners were asked to send the craziest holiday cards in. Every day a listener, who had sent the weirdest one, would get a giant Laser 558 wall poster. July 30th, in the early hours of the morning, it was Ric Harris who told that also a letter from the BBC Monitoring Service was received. He wouldn't comment on the context of the letter but played a song dedicated to the staff of the BBC.

I must not forget to tell how another dinghy was leaving the Communicator to another destination, this time to the coast. It happened on August 1st when the radio ship's dinghy arrived on the beach at Frinton-on-Sea with Laser crew members on board. An accident had happened on the radio ship while Captain Leftwich was using the dinghy winch. He caught a rope round his finger, which was severed. At first, he didn't want to go ashore. Luckily, other crew members made him realise that it was important to seek expert treatment so it was decided to take the dinghy and sail to the beach. They considered calling for a lifeboat but realised that could take about three hours to get to the Communicator.

At Frinton they phoned for an ambulance which took the captain to Colchester Hospital. Dialling '999' meant involving the Police, which was a little tricky. Not only as they came from a radio ship but also two of the crew-members, who accompanied the captain, had no passports with them! They had to report to the Immigration Control the following day, but all went well for them. Officially they got permission to go back to the MV Communicator. However, it would take some days before they could leave as the weather conditions were very rough at the time.

On August 6th they went back to the ship and although the severed finger had been taken ashore, it couldn't be saved. On August 2nd, the captain decided to discharge himself from the hospital and took a plane back to the USA.

My children grew up in those days, being nine, four and three years of age, so I didn't have too much opportunity to listen to Laser 558 late at night. Each day in those years, we had an early start. In my diary I found back some notes from August 7th,1984, when I noted that I heard for the very first time a close-down from the station: 'At 0.100 BST Laser closed down. I heard ABBA singing 'Thank you for the music'. I recorded the close-down and wrote it down and learned later that the programmes normally ended that way.

Next was mentioned: "This is All Europe Radio Laser 5-5-8 broadcasting live from the MV Communicator in international waters. Laser 5-5-8 is owned and operated by Eurad SA and is a totally free environment. At all times this station endeavours to maintain standards of good taste and responsible technical operation. We will resume our transmissions of hit music in a few hours at 5.00 A.M. in the Greenwich Time Zone, 6.00 A.M. in the Central European Time Zone. Thank you for listening today and have a good night."

Being up so late that night, I had problems the next day to fully concentrate on the radio while getting the kids out of bed and have a proper breakfast with them, although they never complained about it.

Meanwhile Martin van der Ven and his family went for a holiday from Germany to Denmark: 'We went some lovely August weeks to a holiday house at the Danish North Sea coast, in Vester Husby, which is in West Jutland. I enjoyed a lot listening to Caroline but the signal from Laser 558 suffered heavy interference from an East German radio station. At home I also didn't have pleasure during the evening listening to the station, so I had to focus myself on cassette recordings, which I got from someone in England.

Mighty Joe Young and
Mike Barrington

Chapter 6

SUMMER 1984

The summer of 1984 brought some new words to the 558 kHz listeners vocabulary, as the Laser DJs often referred to things like 'Eurotan '84' and 'splinter beach'. It was a really good summer with time to get some good tan as well as being on your favourite beach. For those on the MV Communicator the beach could be found on their own deck, filled with wooden splinters.

A special article appeared in the Irish Post newspaper, in which was claimed that Laser 558 was not too much loved by the Irish people in Britain: 'Many thousands of Irish people living in Britain were at the weekend prevented from listening to the RTE radio broadcasting of the Kerry-Cork Munster senior football final because of continuing interference from Laser Radio, a pirate station operating in international waters. The owners of Laser haven't yet been identified. The station is fronted by Music Media International, a marketing company in New York City. Music Media International's President, Roy Lindau, was recently in London – as was Glenn Kolk, a Florida lawyer who act for the owners of the pirate radio station. Glenn Kolk is attached to the law firm of Shutts & Bowen in Miami Florida.

Both Lindau and Kolk defended Laser 558. Kolk, however, promised O'Callaghan that they would consider narrowing the bandwidth that Laser is broadcasting which should reduce the interference. At that time, Radio Laser's two transmitters were temporarily out of action but soon the station was broadcasting as powerful as before, with its interference extending nine kilohertz from 558 to RTE's 576' alleged the Irish Post.

In his exchanges with Jon O'Callaghan, director of RTE, Roy Lindau had made much of RTE not being a British station; of the fact that RTE and Laser transmitters were 400 miles away and that RTE had, at that time, a 500 Kilowatt transmitter, while Laser operated with, at most, only 25 kW. Lindau had also proffered as a solution that RTE could have asked London stations to rebroadcast certain RTE programs.

On August the 5th, Charlie Wolf informed us about his daily pastime reading horoscopes. It brought for him the good news that soon a nice woman had fallen for him. Charlie added that Jessie Brendon was the only woman with whom he was permitted to have a professional relationship; he didn't want any relationship with the groupie, who had recently come aboard the Communicator. The next day we learned that Charlie left the ship for a shore leave.

At that time, we were reminded of the good old days of Radio London when, each weekday, Tony Windsor brought us 'Recipe Time'. On August 8th we heard at 17.30 in the afternoon the ship's cook, Michael Dean, telling listeners about a special recipe, which was sent in by a listener from Leigh. That's a small seaside place near Southend so fish was one of the ingredients. A small article in the Observer on the 9th August it was mentioned that Laser's office in New York was claiming an average listenership of 6 million people a day in England, France, Belgium, Holland and Germany.

Four days later, we saw the return of Charlie Wolf who immediately took over his own slot between 9pm and 1am. After five days shore leave a lot of listeners were happy when he returned, with his zany kind of humour, which his shows were full of. On August 14th another press report came from the New York office from Music Media International. Although it was yet five weeks before the end of the summer of 1984, the press report said: 'This has been a very special summer for Laser listeners because it has been completely commercial free. The decision to run a summer of commercial free programming was made by MMI President Roy Lindau. He claimed: "I wanted to establish credibility and build a large audience quickly; audiences respond to limited commercials."

I thought that if the idea of a commercial free summer came from the brains of Roy Lindau, wasn't this another problem for the station manager? Were the promised international companies too afraid to bring their products into the European market by advertising on Laser 558? On the other hand, by following Laser's results they should have realised that the station was really a hit, as newspapers said more than once that Laser 558 took listeners away from stations like BBC Radio One and Capital Radio. Headlines mentioned daily that Laser 558 had over 5 million listeners but remember that sometimes they differ from the true facts. The New York office promised that in

September 1984 a poll would be held in Britain and two other countries.

Lindau, however, seemed to believe in more than pure reality by stating: "We have inquiries from advertisers as far away as Australia who are interested in placing ad's on Laser 558, since the station is reaching nine countries in north western Europe, including the United Kingdom, the Netherlands, Denmark, France and Germany. Commercial prices range from $40 to $250 dollars for a 30 seconds spot. Sponsors can have their commercial booked in New York offices and aired the same day in Europe, due to the fact we have a professional satellite link to our radio ship, the MV Communicator.'"

Was the statement from Roy Lindau a perfect way to say: 'Sorry, we don't have any advertisers, the sun is shining and we all enjoy doing our thing to bring you the best radio station in the world where the music is never more than a minute away?' Earlier statements from the New York offices told us that soon many international advertisers could be heard in the programmes. Commercial time on the station could be brought in as the station had an American office where airtime could be booked, American staff and deejays and so was not subject to the Marine Offences Act. Probably a very expensive attorney should have looked at the influence of the MOA on the running of the station. However, in mid-August there were no advertisers and I started wondering what Roy Lindau meant when he used the word 'soon'.

August 15th brought a generator breakdown and so the station was off the air from 13.30 till around 16.00 hrs. We learned that after a long period, transmitter technician Mighty Joe Young was back on the radio ship. Now and then he could be heard during 'off the air hours', when he put the transmitter on for some time.

On August 18th a further front page story appeared in the Irish Post. 'RTE listeners in Britain trying to dial away from the interference of Laser now finish up with Radio Caroline.' Glen Kolk, the Miami lawyer, who represents the owners of Radio Laser. He assured this newspaper that filters were about to be installed which would eliminate the interference with RTE, by cutting off Radio Laser's sideband at 4.5 kHz beyond 558. "This should leave RTE radio clear of interference', he said.

Also in the Irish Post was a mentioning of the fact Laser still had no commercials and also this time Lindau was asked for a reason: "We're confident of lining up advertisers within a matter of weeks and have hopes of being profitable by Christmas."

Like many others, I had the opinion that Lindau played the role of braggart at that stage. Luckily, he didn't say which Christmas! Everyone knowing a little about the radio industry, and especially radio from a ship in international waters, knows that it cost a lot building up and running a station. This cannot be earned back within four months with some international advertisers. Around August 1984 the running costs of Laser were around 15,000 pounds sterling every week. This included pay for the eleven crew and the daily food supply. To avoid breaching the MOA, Laser needed to receive its supplies from a country that was not a signatory to the 1965 'European Agreement for the Prevention of Broadcasts from Stations Outside National Territory', the also called Strasburg Agreement.

More than a quarter of a century later we know of course that the Communicator, Laser's vessel, as well as the Ross Revenge, were tendered by ships from several harbours, mostly from the countries who signed the above mentioned agreement. In the summer of 1984 several people in the Laser organisation insisted that the Communicator was serviced from the harbour of El Ferrol, in the north of Spain. In the first year of Laser 558 in international waters, this didn't happen and the small tenders came from a harbour in the Isle of Sheppey.

August 19th brought us again some breakdowns due to technical problems and it seemed just right for Holly Michaels who had slept badly during the past days. She also cheered up a bit by cook Michael Dean, who concocted what he called a 'Staying Alive juice' during her programme.

August also saw the first lines in the news that the big Capital Radio, one of the ILR stations in the Greater London area, was becoming concerned about a steady loss of listeners who had retuned their radio to 558 kHz. It also became known that the frequency of '558' had been given to a local BBC station in Essex.

Laser stayed in the headlines in several newspapers: 'Man from the BBC linked with pop pirate ship' was the headline above an article in 'The Standard' on August 21st. It suggested that a top BBC TV journalist was one of the people behind the setting up of a powerful radio ship in the North Sea. The name of Roger Parry, a regular reporter on BBC TV News programmes, was mentioned. Roger himself however strongly denied anything to do with the project. An investigation by journalists of the London 'Standard' had uncovered strong evidence that Roger Parry acted as a coordinator of the project, designed to establish the station Laser 558 as a direct competitor of BBC and Independent radio stations ashore.

Some journalists wrote in depth about the MOA and it was reported that Parry had already been interviewed by Police about his involvement with Laser 558. Journalists went on to report that four people, who were involved with the setting up of the station, had told the police that Parry had been the adviser as well as the coordinator. They said that the owner of an American company, who supplied electronic equipment to the MV Communicator, had said that he had dealt with Parry on contractual matters.

Contrary to the claim that the highly professional but unlicensed station was American backed, the Standard brought the fact that inquiries showed that all the money came from the Republic of Ireland. One rich entrepreneur in particular was mentioned: 'One of Scotland Yard's top investigative teams was to look into the activities of Laser 558 in conjunctions with investigators from the Department of Trade and Industry. At present police are waiting for authority from the Director of Public Prosecutions to widen the scope of their investigations. '

Parry himself was also interviewed by an Evening Standard journalist and stated repeatedly that the suggestions were bizarre and nonsense. He added that he was investigating the activities of the Laser organisation as a journalist for a possible article for 'In Business', where he was one of the editorial team. He had interviewed station marketing chief Lindau and met him on several occasions in that context but had not had any hand in setting up the station. But several people, who had at that stage no longer connections to Laser, told the journalist that they took orders from Parry.

Meanwhile the newspaper could name another person with a British passport who had worked by setting up of the station and who we had heard already during one of the test transmissions: Paul Rusling.

He admitted helping to supervise the setting up of the station and went to Florida to kit out the ship with modern studio and transmission equipment. Some weeks later, the book 'The Lid off Laser 558' was published in England written by the same Paul Rusling. In chapter three of his book, Rusling stated: "One of the backer's closest advisers was a man who was involved with the BBC on the news and production." To the journalist from the Irish Post Rusling refused to mention the names of the adviser or the owner, only mentioning that it was an Irishman. For more about this subject, I advise you to read 'The Lid off Laser 558' by Paul Rusling.

When talking to the editor of Monitor Magazine, Buster Pearson, Rusling confirmed the same month that Parry was the man he was referring to as 'the adviser': "When he was with us, he used to walk around with his coat turned up and a strange hat on, in the case anyone recognised him. He has been completely in charge on more than one occasion."

For me still the question raised why the name 'Parry' was so important for the journalist of the Irish Post. Was it just because he originated from Ireland? But soon more was revealed.

August 24th, the start of a weekend with glory for the Laser Road Show as in six different places they did a gig. One of them was a so called 'Fifties Night' including a competition where a weekend in Paris was to be won. Another show, held in Ashford, gave a trial in which the world record for a motor jumping through fire was attempted.

Another connection to Ireland was published in the London Evening Standard on August 30th: 'A wealthy Irish hotel and disco entrepreneur was the man who helped to finance the setting up of a powerful pirate radio ship known as Laser 558. Philip Smyth's key role has been kept a closely guarded secret. He operated through financial 'advisers' including his personal friend Roger Parry, a BBC newsman.'

An investigation by The Standard had shown that Smyth was the mystery boss of Laser 558 in operation – designed to make a killing out of U.S. advertising: "So far it is believed that more than two million dollars has been pumped into the project, all from Philip Smyth. His involvement will be of great interest to the Irish Government and his broadcasting organisation Radio Telefis Eireann." The board of directors of RTE already had complained to the British government about interference from Laser 558 with RTE's Radio One.

Philip Smyth, being an Irish citizen, did not commit any offence under British law at that stage. Smyth's involvement with Laser 558 only came to light by accident, when the police in Sheerness were arresting one of Laser's captains, David Irvine from Arizona. He was fined 500 Pounds for an offence under the MOA of supply equipment for an offshore radio station while in the UK. Among his possessions seized by the local police was a letter of appointment from the organisation, which was signed by Irishman Philip Smyth. That letter was signed in April, while the ship was being fitted with a new aerial. In the months after Irving's arrest, many people involved with the station were questioned and gave confirmation Smyth's involvement.

A few days later, the London Standard reported that Roger Parry was the adviser and administrator for Philip Smyth. Journalists of the newspaper tried to contact Smyth on the telephone number of the Sachs Hotel that he owned in Dublin. The receptionist would not tell where he was at that moment and was reluctant to take a message. Research showed that he lived, at that stage, in Fox Rock, a leafy and expensive Dublin suburb. His house, then worth around 200,000 Pounds, was surrounded by well-tended grounds and a security wall.

What was the influence of Laser 558 after just three months of broadcasting from international waters, with a lot of breakdowns and other problems? Well, the ILR stations were getting very anxious at losing a lot of listeners to the new offshore station and also those responsible at BBC Radio One got nervous with the new sound. But the most influence Laser 558 had was on the sound of Radio Caroline, their neighbour in international waters. Listeners to both two stations learned that at the end of August Radio Caroline sounded far much like a pop station, with the new hits and golden oldies then they had before, with their all-album format. Caroline really tried their utmost to be a competitor for Laser 558.

September 1984 started and on the Laser ship were some changes. On the 3rd Tommy 'What a guy' Rivers came back on the MV Communicator after a spell on shore of only six days. For Jessie Brandon, the next day was terrible. A North Sea gale was brewing and she became increasingly seasick. Luckily enough, the last half hour of her show was taken over by Mighty Joe Young. This was the first time we heard him live on air and we wrote down in our logbook that we liked him for he had come over as a top class broadcaster.

September 6th gave us 'a first', mentioning that for the first time promos were aired on Laser 558 for the Dutch version of the Laser Road Show. It had already made several appearances in England. September 8th brought us also a new program, called 'The Zany Hour', which was broadcast on weekend nights between 01.00 and 0.200. It was presented by any of the ship's crew that could stay awake and anything could happen in the program. A pity that it was scheduled so late, as more would enjoy it earlier in the day. This was to become a regularly weekend feature and was proving extremely popular with Laser listeners. Each week the program had an open end and mostly the length was extended to two or more hours. On the 15th September we heard for example Chris Allan, who was at that stage a ships engineer, being assisted by the Sea Wolf.

Some household messages were mentioned on air, that many loved to hear on other offshore radio stations. Listeners were informed on September 16th that Jessie Brandon had one of her wisdom teeth coming through which was causing severe tooth pain. She was a good girl and persevered to present her program between 17.00 and 21.00 hours that same day. Summer ended with the return of Paul Dean on Laser, after a long period of absence.

Paul Dean

Chapter 7

A COURT CASE

On September 13th we heard for the first time on Laser 558 that one more hour would be added to the weekend programming, now continuing till 02.00 BST. During this late programme, so they promised, a guest would appear; it turned out to be a crewmember, accompanied by Charlie Wolf. A day later Holly Michaels said that Charlie was restless as he jumped out of bed at a very early time, thinking the tender would come alongside to take him to 'Spain'.

A few days later, September 17th, it became known that one of the most important ILR stations, Capital Radio, had lost 1 million listeners since the success of Laser 558 became more known to more and more people. As a result of that the management decided to change format and it sounded then very near to the Laser 558 sound, though still with the needle time restrictions. Capital also said goodbye to some of their deejays, including former Big L and RNI deejay Duncan Johnson.

September 20th, we heard from one of our sources that the British Government complained about Inmarsat, the international organisation controlling in those days the use of satellite connections. They wanted to bring an official protest that an illegal radio station was using satellite equipment. Lindau on the phone from New York had a big laugh and told that he wasn't afraid of such an action. However, he told that when in the then forthcoming December not enough advertisers were booked there were a few suggestions made for the future: 1) stop broadcasting 2) starting religious programming and 3) selling airtime to other radio organisations. That there were problems over advertising, we could hear on the air, when Ric Harris screamed in his show: "Advertisers where are you?"

September 21st saw Charlie going away for a leave and Jessie taking over his program, in which she had an interesting talk with Paul Dean about personality radio and radio personalities. A day later it was Paul Dean himself presenting the late night programming on 558.

In the meantime, a new name was introduced in the organisation, 'John Catlett'. Who was he and did he have a role in radio before? He was one of the many people attending 'Driftback 20' a radio convention held in the Boddington Hotel in Russel Square in Central London in 1987. It was Chris Edwards who interviewed Catlett and asked him when he was involved in radio for the first time. He got a surprising answer:

"My first involvement with radio was to take part in a radio play way back in 1943, when I was two years of age. I had a small part in the play, so I was told. That was such a resounding success that I decided in 1960 to join my college radio FM station at Princetown University which was operating commercially by the students. It had also an AM channel serving the university campus and I worked there as a classical announcer, as news reporter, news director and went on to be advertising manager as well as business manager. I spent the summers working professionally for American commercial radio stations in towns near my home in Ashland, Ohio."

John Catlett, Station Manager

That was where a long career in radio began for John Catlett and several decades later he was at the Madison Avenue offices of Laser 558. How did he get involved? "Over a period of time I purchased my own radio station in Hartford, Connecticut, with a group of investors from the Hartford area, which is about 100 miles from New York. My partners were mostly black and the station specifically appealed to a black audience even though it had been owned by a white man and had the black format. I managed that for two or three years and I had a sales manager whom I hired and trained and was ready to take over. He was also black and better qualified to manage the station. When I left the station, I taught marketing at the University of Connecticut for one year and then accepted a consulting assignment for a month for a friend, who had once worked with me briefly. He was trying to sort out the management problems of trying to run a radio station in the North Sea."

How did the contact between Catlett and Laser started? ' It happened through young guy, Scott Randall, had worked at one time as a secretary for me and we stayed in contact. His wife was an artist and I bought some paintings from her. He told me about the project he was working on for Laser. He was producing the advertising and promotional materials for the station because he was then running his own little advertising agency and he knew Roy Lindau, who had hired him to do the materials. Scott told me about Lindau and the structure of Laser, such as it was, and invited me to take a look at it to see if I could suggest ways to straighten out the management problems that were going on."

"After looking at it, my analysis was that the station was being run by a sales manager in New York, a marine attorney in Florida and a marine supplier in England. Each one thought that they were running the entire operation as was the captain of the ship, but none of those people had run a radio station before. My recommendation essentially was that someone be hired to run the radio station, who had done that sort of thing before, who was willing to live on board a ship and somewhere within the listening area of the station and occasionally visit the sales office in New York and I volunteered."

On September 24th, 1984 a newsflash was brought on TVS 'Coast to Coast': "The owner of a shipping firm at Sheerness has been cleared of supplying goods to a pirate radio station. Nicholas Murray of the isle of Sheppey pleaded 'not guilty' at Maidstone Crown Court to conspiring to supply antenna masts to the motor vessel Communicator, the Radio Laser ship anchored off the Essex coast. The Prosecution offered no evidence after it was found that a legal textbook, on which the charges were based, contained a misprint. The judge directed a verdict of not guilty be entered."

Two days later a small piece could be read in 'Campaign' which is a weekly newspaper for the advertising market in the UK: "Capital Radio is trying to poach one of the star DJs of the North Sea pirate station, Laser 558. Capital's program director, Jo Sandilands, who just adopted a more youth-oriented policy, has written to Jessie Brandon, one of Laser's five American presenters, offering 'lots of money' if Brandon will work for Capital in the five-to- seven o'clock slot each evening." Jessie did later join Capital, but the government refused a work permit, so she had to make the programmes at a studio in New York, with a Capital producer, who then flew the tapes across to London for transmission.

On September 24th, the Essex Police visited a Laser Lover Road Show. They thought there was illegal transmitting equipment at the venue, possibly an offence of the Wireless Telegraphy Act, 1949.

Two days later we heard from Lindau that a lot of advertisers were booked for transmission in October. 'The spots are already on the computer and ready to be aired.' We made a note and hoped nobody would use the 'clear button' on the computer! On September 27th the first mentioning of a Laser Lover Roadshow, to be held in the Netherlands, was promoted: It was to be staged on October 5th in Sliedrecht, with a performance by Dutch singer Vanessa.

On September 28th we heard the return of 'Stoner'. David Lee came back after a 42 days ashore, but he had earned his holiday as he had joined the project almost a year before in Florida and had sailed across the Atlantic Ocean with the ship. A day later we heard the first announcement about a 'Laser Sticker Kit' and the next day we heard the female deejay Holly Michaels. During her show, that went out between 21.00 and 01.00 hours she was assisted by the Captain of the Communicator, Tim Levensaler. Holly Michaels also came from the USA, Minneapolis to be exactly. She had been working during two years before on station KKBJ in Bemedji, after completing her broadcast training at the Brown Institute.

In the USA, people who try to get a career in radio or television, often first try to get a degree in broadcasting at a university. Holly chose the Brown College which is a profit making school and a subsidiary of Career Education Corporation. It's located in Mendota Heights, Minnesota, near Minneapolis. Brown College offers programs in the areas of Broadcasting, Design, Technology and Management. Communication studies is an academic field in the USA that deals with processes of sharing over distances in space and time. Hence, communication studies encompass a wide range of topics and contexts ranging from face-to- face conversation to speeches to mass media outlets such as television broadcasting. Communication Studies, as a discipline, is also often interested in how audiences interpret information and the political, cultural, economic, and social dimensions of speech and language in context.

September 29th, 1984 the bad news came in that a petrol bomb was thrown into the Punch Tavern, in Whitstable. It was the pub owned by Paul Alexander Rusling, who was involved with Laser during the early days of the project. He wrote a book about his time with the organisation and how the station was built. Not everybody was happy with his book 'The Lid off Laser 558' and rumours soon spread around that the bomb was thrown by someone acting for the Laser organisation. For more on 'The Lid of Laser' read Rusling's book.

The 29th of September brought us David Lee Stone and Holly Michaels during the late evening program talking about a journey, they made together during shore leave, through 14 different European countries. The next day it seemed there were problems with the generator as the music was distorted. Later, the station went off the air and in evening the second transmitter came on the air and Holly Michaels did some test announcements, which went on till 04.00. The next morning the other transmitter was back with low power and bad modulation.

Memories fade so let's try to remember the rundown of a daily program schedule of Laser 558, this time from October 1st, 1984: The day started with a program from Ric Harris, which had duration of five hours, beginning at 5.00 o'clock in the morning. A long stint, as were the following programs. David Lee Stone was on air till 15.00 hours and Tommy Rivers was the third deejay of the day ending his show at 20.00 hours. Then another five hours show with Holly till 01.00 in the night. Jessie Brandon had departed for a holiday and no replacement arrived on the Communicator, which the reason for shifts of five hours. We were surprised to hear that day commercials for Ski Magazine, Ashwin Fire Extinguishers and The Lost Opera, so Lindau, on that occasion at least, was to be trusted! (Later it transpired that the adverts had been obtained via the London agent, Rob Day, and not Lindau at all.).

The Lost Opera was an album by the Korean soprano Kimera and the Operaiders with the London Symphony Orchestra. Consisting of snatches of popular operatic arias and choruses against a disco beat, in the style of Hooked on Classics, it was released by the record label Red Bus. Whilst highly promoted on Laser 558 it was not a major UK success. It spent some sixteen weeks in the French charts. The LP was repackaged in a style more disco than classical in 1985 and reissued with the title "Hits On Opera", and with a more techno style cover illustration, but gaining little additional interest.

Who was the Laser deejay Tommy Rivers? In 1994 Chris Edwards from Offshore Echos Magazine interviewed Tommy and he answered with: "I grew up as a kid in a little mining town in northern Minnesota near the Canadian border and all we had on the local radio was polkas, radio bingo and ice-hockey play-by-play. We moved to Minneapolis in the early sixties and at that time there two Top 40 stations going crazy. I thought that radio was magic and I wanted to work in it from day one. So, I got out of high school and went in to the two first years of college and I wanted to go into fisheries and wild-life management. But there were no jobs then so I thought to hell with them, I'll do what I really want to do and go in to radio, which I did in 1976 at WWTC News Radio 1280 in Minneapolis."

It was there that Tommy Rivers learned an important aspect of working in radio, which was reading the news. On April 15th, 1976 he got his first real job op WTMBA-FM, from which he remembered: "a real exciting place. Then I went to KRSI Radio, AM and FM in Minneapolis. It was 1980 and became their morning news reporter. That station became KJJO-FM 104 in 1981 in which I was the overnight jock on modern country, a kicking country station. That was my bull-riding and bear-wrestling days. In 1983 that station went to oldies rock and roll, which was very similar in music terms as Virgin Radio 1215 now."

"Then I saw an ad' in a trade paper which said "work on the largest radio station in Europe!" It didn't say anything about a ship and I had just finished my master's degree at the University of Minnesota in audience research and I thought what the heck this sounds pretty good, sent a tape and a C.V. away and didn't think anything on it. Lindau called me from New York and asked would I be interested in this job. He told me what it was all about and that it was on a ship. I said that this was bizarre because my college adviser was like the American expert on the whole pirate scene so I knew about these things unlike some of the other guys."

"Lindau flew out to Minneapolis and asked when I could I start and I told him about two weeks. He told me the salary and I said that was pretty low so he asked if I wanted to become operations manager, which doubled my income and so I thought to go. Two weeks later I was on the plane to Miami and spent three days with Glenn Kolk, who was our marine lawyer that dealt with the Panamanian registry. Next, I flew to New York for two or three days on Madison Avenue and met the staff there and after that I flew over here and was on the air early June 1984, about two weeks into the run of Laser at that time."

Imagine that you're were dreaming of a career at Europe's biggest station and just days before you'll hear that it is based on a ship in international waters. What an impact this must have on your life. Living together with about 15 other people on the ship, who were coming from all kind of places, having all their own behaviour as well as their ups and downs.

What was Tommy River's first impression when he arrived? "When we first arrived it was cool. We were on this tugboat and it was misty and we seemed to be going for days. We eventually got out there at three in the morning and you'd see these glowing lights in the distance and it looked pretty impressive like a Spanish galleon until you came alongside and it's this rusty bucket. You scratch your head and say: 'What the hell have I gotten myself into? And then you climb up the rope and the next day on the air and that's the way it was. Very few of us got sick out there and that was the best way, just to muck in and start doing it."

A new commercial was played for a Laser Road Show touring the Netherlands with DJ Frans van der Drift. In the seventies he worked with for Radio Mi Amigo and in 1984 told us that he didn't ask for promotion on Laser 558 but that the people behind the station liked it so much that they decided to give the road show free plugs.

Chapter 8

COAST TO COAST

During the month of October 1984 there was publicity for Laser 558 on the local as well as on national television. First an 11 minute feature was transmitted by TVS Local News. They sent out a crew including a former offshore deejay, Alan Clark, who had worked for Radio City on Shivering Sands Fort. He interviewed the crew and deejays for the program 'Coast to Coast', including Holly Michaels, Tom Levansaler, Charlie Wolf and Jessie Brendon. It was told by them that once a month they got a tender from Spain and that they were very proud that in this way they were a legal radio station.

Also, Holly Michaels added that they all got along well and that it was a kind of family situation on the Communicator. Well, in all families there's sometimes trouble too! This item was transmitted on the 1st of October. Over half of the feature was taken up with an interview with Paul Rusling, about his book The Lid Off Laser 558' and his involvement building the radio station into the Communicator.

Two days later, ITN's national bulletin 'News at One' interviewed Roy Lindau, who said: 'We want world-class advertisers and we're not seeking British advertisers or British companies. Everybody loves to call us 'pirates' but we really are not illegal. We're an operation in international waters which are one of the freest areas on earth. No one has ever asked us to pay a licence fee. If someone sends us a bill, we'll consider it. There is no licensing authority at sea. I think there is a marketing hole. I'm in marketing and I think there are a lot of people who want a full-time music service so we're providing it.'

On October 9th Jessie Brandon and Charlie Wolfe returned to the station, both after a short holiday. Charlie had taken with him a record that since became his regular theme tune. The story goes that he found this most appropriate ditty amongst a pile of platters in a junk shop! Entitled 'Who's afraid of the Big Bad Wolf' his jingle was taken from the Walt Disney's story of the Three Little Pigs, which was issued in 1967 on the Disney record label.

More publicity came in the Daily Mail with a story about Jessie Brandon joining Capital Radio. They taped some of her shows and were offering her own shows on the station as she speaks Russian, has a degree in journalism and broadcasting, and has worked on 13 American radio stations. "I'm a radio gypsy and I've worked on rock stations, country stations, and middle of the road stations. I was a deejay on WOMN, a soft rock feminist station in the States. When I joined Laser, I became the only woman among about 15 men. Now I'm music director and we've got one more woman deejay here. Thank goodness!"

The newspaper was talking about Holly Michaels who went for a well-earned holiday on October 12th and was replaced by newcomer Dave Chaney, who came from San Francisco, but was originally born in Australia. The month October also brought new commercials for 'USA Today' and 'Marlboro Rock across America'. The month also saw some days of bad weather and Charlie Wolf loved to show it to his listeners. One day he held the microphone through the porthole so we could hear the storm raging outside.

David Chaney

October 13th, we heard for the first time a very professional promo for buying airtime on the station, in which the local shop owner was advised to get airtime of his local radio station while the big fishes were advised to get in contact with Music Media International in New York. Around that time MMI also began using a postal address in The Hague (PO Box 82314), in the Netherlands.

Vincent Monsey, the President of Radio Caroline in those days, told us about the special deal with USA Today on October 15th: "Roy Lindau won't ask for any money playing this commercial within the Laser 558 programming. There's s special deal whereby 'USA Today' gets free airtime and Music Media International gets free advertisement space in the newspaper so the organisation can try to get big advertisers interested. It's a $25,000 deal."

"The editor from Ski Magazine is one of Roy Lindau's friends and the commercial on Laser was aired for free. If any new subscribers joined from Europe a small commission would be paid."

After some normal days of programming, October 23rd was a busy day, for David Lee Stone as he suddenly had to take over from a new deejay, David Chaney, who was taken ill and had to get into his bunk. It is not known exactly when he came on board the Communicator for the first time.

On October 24th it was birthday time on the Communicator as David Lee Stone became a year older. His colleagues made some fun out of it to tell the listener that it was his sixty-fifth birthday. On board the Ross Revenge, Caroline's radio ship, they also dedicated a song to Stoner's for his birthday. David Chaney was also celebrating his birthday and was feeling far much better than the day before. From October 27th dedications played on Laser 558 got a new name as they were called 'Lasergrams'. The 28th saw an unusual item; the start of the TBS (A bank corporation) Rock School Competition. The winner was promised to get airplays on Laser 558 as well as on BBC Radio 1.

At the end of the month, as well during the first days of November, some new advert's were heard in the shows: Consolidated International, a supplier of industrial parts. Also, a commercial for a newspaper called 'Ritz' was heard and one for 'Bose' loudspeakers.

Promotion for the movie 'Red Dawn' followed, about a group of children calling themselves 'the Wolverlines'. October 30th, 1984, I read an article about Laser in a German Magazine, Der Stern, in which there were several rumours were built around the organisation. One of the things suggested was that the Communicator was a 'staging point' for hashish smuggling. Other rumours were that the station was financed and owned by the IRA and there was one that the ship was owned by the Bahgwan.

The report also mentioned that an official complaint was made by the technical director of the Deutschlandfunk in Cologne, Werner Hinz. He had written a letter to the Director of the West German Ministry, responsible for the use of frequencies, and complained that Laser 558 had several times interfered with the frequencies of the German station. Martin van der Ven commented: 'I think that the interference mentioned was with the transmitter from Deutschlandfunk in Nordkirchen. For me there were reception problems the other way round; Deutschlandfunk's big transmitter interfered with Laser!

November 2nd, I wrote down that Ric Harris played a special song for 'the Toad'. The song he played started with the line: 'You got a nerve to call us your friends'. Suggestions were made that the Toad was Paul Alexander Rusling and copies of his book were read on the ship. Three days later we heard again, after a long time, a commercial for a Laser Lover Road Show, however without the name of the deejay Robbie Day. The commercial for the Dutch Laser Road Show on November the 6th gave the name of Nico van der Steen as deejay. He was later involved in Radio Monique, a sister station to Radio Caroline, also transmitting from the MV Ross Revenge.

On November 7th the first commercial was heard for 'Rolling Stone' the music trade magazine from the USA, which was also available in shops around Western Europe. Three days later it was another new commercial for 'Spann crackers'. It was Tom de Munck of the Freewave Media Magazine who advised the people on the New York office early in November to pay attention to Remembrance Day, which is held every year on November 11th. And it resulted in two minutes silence on Laser 558 at 12.00 that day in respect of all those who died during the wars in which Britons were involved. On November 12th, rumours were spread around that Laser 558 could become soon an all English station, whereby 'goodbye' would be given to the American deejays. It was stated that this could bring more advertisers to the station.

Two tenders in two days seems to be an expensive thing for an organisation'. A reader wrote to me that he didn't understand that when an announcement came, for instant on November 13th, 1984, that Charlie Wolf was on leave, and that the next day suddenly Holly Michaels was back, both with the same tender. Holly was back after a holiday of 33 days, which she enjoyed in San Diego.

Around that time also a new contest started to mark the inauguration of 'Virgin Airlines' new route between Maastricht (in the south of the Netherlands) and Gatwick Airport. Free return tickets were offered as prizes. Listeners, who wanted to participate in the contest, had to answer three questions: two about the then current all-hit music scene and one about the construction of the Maastricht Airport.

As I told earlier the name of BBC1 was mentioned in the commercial for TBS Rock School together with the one of Laser 558. That asked for more and followed first in the so called 'Ad Lib' column from the newspaper London Standard on November 13th: ' A boob by a bank means blushes at the Beeb. The Beeb and the TBS are jointly organising a schools rock competition and an advertisement for the contest began being broadcast on Laser last week. This is particularly embarrassing since British companies are forbidden by law from advertising on pirate radio stations. Laser devised the commercial after being sent a press release from the bank. 'We aren't paying for the ad' and we've asked Laser to stop playing it', admits a TBS person. Over at the Department of Trade and Industry, the British governmental pirate radio watchdogs, they're not amused. 'Frankly we're surprised that the TBS should send a press release to an illegal organisation,' sniffs a spokeswoman.'

November 14th Jessie Brandon played some of the winning commercials from CLIO Awards; they brought a special colour to her programme. We didn't follow Laser closely during early November but discovered that on the 14th, Holly Michaels, who was on shore leave, returned to give Charlie a well-earned shore leave.

The Time Magazine of November 15th had an article related to Laser 558 featuring Charlie Wolf, who was interviewed by reporter John Marshall: 'Laser's Charlie Wolf is anything but all at sea. Charlie Wolf, like many radio jocks, is not quite what you might expect. He is a tee-total, non-smoking 25 year old, former Jewish now Mormon, formerly Bostonian, now living in the middle of the North Sea. Wolf's been with Laser 558 for three months, before which he was pumping out country music and adult contemporary rock to the good folks of Provo, Utah and Salt Lake City. The move to the water gave him an audience of well over five million, though it doesn't feel always like that. 'The problem is feedback. Out there on the ship we don't get to meet our audience. Letters are the only contact and they take time to get through'.

When we met recently in a well-known pub in the Capital City, every question of mine was countered with a fast answer by him. 'What do we sound like to you?' and 'who's listening?' and 'what do they all think?' The answers: 'Good', 'large numbers' and 'they like it a lot' never seemed to satisfy'. After John Marshall related additional information about the Communicator he went on with: 'On summer weekend charter boats come out to circle the ship. Listeners are snapping away their instamatics and shouting greetings and tossing the odd fresh newspaper on board. Occasionally working boats are passing by, or got in touch, like the fishing boat which needed some bread and got in Laser in return for a flounder. '

And about the station's policy: 'Laser leave little room for the presenters to project themselves. The policy of being never more away than a minute from the music means that pace and style has to be built through the music itself and the odd few words in between.

"There's a golden rule in radio', told Wolf, 'if you got something to say, keep it short, if not - keep the microphone closed'. It's a good rule and one which has probably contributed more than anything else to Laser's success.' Charlie had also something more to say how you could bring the program on a higher level: '"For me it's the Fever Pitch, building the pace record by record, link by link until it reaches high tension, then letting things calm down a little before building it to the next peak. It's a keenness and edge on air which is all the more impressive for the lack of stimulants required to feed it. It comes straight from the music itself, from a feel from people enjoying themselves harmlessly, and honestly. And it works!"

The humour we heard a lot in Charlie's program was also to be read in the article in Time Out: "Her Majesty's Government, of course, is not amused. Still under the illusion that Laser is breaking some law there is little doubt they would like to send a missile on the course for the North Sea. They should beware. If memory serves well, Exocets can be stopped by Seawolves.'

Listeners were happy too as mots of mail came to the ship, via the New York office and listeners also wrote into the regular offshore related magazines like: Freewave Media Magazine, Monitor Magazine and OEM. For instant John Kerswill in Surrey, who wrote: "'It's just like old times with the popularity of Laser, you just have to walk through the West End and every shop seems to have Laser on.

I never thought it should happen but Laser at present has certainly caught people's attention. I hope it lasts!'

And strangely enough more people who tuned in regularly to the offshore stations in the Sixties of last century found their way back to their tranny, as Rob van Dijk from Schoorl in the Netherlands wrote: 'Strangely enough I recently heard that a new radio station came on the air, bringing back the memories to Swinging Radio England, fast and up-tempo radio. I heard it from a friend and my transistor is tuned to 558 constantly.'

A third one came from Tim Scrimshaw from Birmingham, who wrote: 'I quite like the bouncy sound from Laser, much better to listen to in the car than to Radio One. For regular listeners Caroline cannot be bettered. For the few days earlier this year both stations were off the air there was really nothing on the radio worth listening to!' Tim later became a deejay himself on the Voice of Peace.

Two days later, November 17th, Ronan O'Rahilly, spokesman for the Caroline organisation probably had a bad dream as he told Tom de Munck that Laser had a spy within the Caroline organisation. This due to the fact, that the commercials for Rolling Stone Magazine originally were planned on Radio Caroline. On hearing the words of O'Rahilly, Lindau offered the first 25 commercials free , winning the spots for Laser 558. Ronan claimed that Laser was only there so the ship could be used as a platform for the CIA. From the New York office there was no comment and the only thing they wanted to add was: "The rumours, which were spread around in Europe that we will going all English with English deejays, is nonsense. No English resident will be hired to be a deejay." The same day another tender and Ric Harris left the ship, David Lee Stone taking over his morning show. Once again, all the deejays presented five hour long shows.

Some changes in programming occurred too after a tender came alongside and so on November 19th the schedule was: 05.00 – 09.00 Tommy Rivers followed by Holly Michaels till 13.00. Then 13.00 - 17.00 David Lee Stone, 17.00-21.00 Jessie Brandon and 21.00-01.00 Charlie Wolf. November 20th began another competition, the Laser/Kontiki America Getaway. Competitors had to send a postcard answering two simple questions: 'What is your favourite radio station?' and 'do you prefer a holiday in the east or the west of America? The listeners first drawn would win a holiday to the USA.

November 20th also saw the return of Tommy Rivers, who had been away so long that listeners thought he might not return to Laser 558. For 43 days he was away. Charlie returned after only 6 days ashore, while David Chaney left the Communicator. One who tuned into the 558 could hear also more and more promo spots. On Sundays the 'Sixties Sunday' was still on the air and the regular concert promotions on the station were credited by 'Time Out Magazine'. Strange that 27 years later, when being in London a few times a year and seeing a copy of this magazine, I directly think about those good old days of Laser 558.

Laser DJs climb the satellite pedestal

In Chris Edwards' interview with Tommy Rivers, he asked him what his first job was on Laser. He knew that Rivers became Programme Director and so Tommy answered: "At the beginning we didn't have a PD, we had a post of Operations Manager, which meant I had to stay in communication with Lindau, writing reports up and basically maintain mechanical scheduling. At that time, they were trying manage the music from New York, believe it or not."

During the early days, even when no test transmissions were aired, the organisation informed us from their New York post offices that a satellite connection would feed the people on the ship with daily fresh information and even 'new music'.

Tommy Rivers was asked if the satellite dome was used: "No, because someone had sabotaged the satellite. We were supposed to use this satellite link but a disgruntled little person as I understand disabled the satellite before I got out there. But at this time, we were using a scrambler to a person on land to order records, supplies, personal effects etc. Then about late 1984, we decided we needed a Programme Director so David Lee Stone became PD for about two or three months and then he went to Radio Luxembourg and John Catlett told me to take over as Programme Director, which I agreed to and I did for most in 1985."

November 21st was Thanksgiving Day in the USA and as Laser 558 was an American organised radio station the deejays paid attention to this with a little celebration dinner party during the Charlie Wolf program. One of the things he played was the album track 'Alice's Restaurant' from Arlo Guthrie. As this LP was not on the Communicator, he had earlier visited the MV Ross Revenge to get a copy of the LP and during his programme, which he presented together with Mighty Joe Young, he thanked the boys at the Banana Republic Caroline.

A day later we had Lindau again on the phone with more promises. He told us: "Soon a lot of multi nationals will advertise on the station, starting with a massive campaign for the International Herald Tribune. And from December Laser will also have the weekly American Top 40 Countdown, a syndicate programme presented by Casey Kasem. It will be aired twice as we want it for our listeners on Saturdays as well as on Sundays."

Chapter 9

PLAYING WITH JOURNALISTS

Charlie often tried to make fun with the newspapers as well as the journalists. It was Friday 23rd of November that Laser went off the air, due to the heavy storm. Listeners however heard Jessie Brandon saying that the station went off the air for maintenance. The power was not more than 7 kW during the day and just before 19.00 the transmitter went off the air, not to come back the same day. Early Sunday morning no signal was heard on 558 so we tuned to competitor Caroline. In their programme they spoke about some problems over on the Communicator and they wished them all a lot of success, playing 'Silence is golden' by the Tremeloes.

Later the day, at 17.19, Laser 558 was back on the air and I heard David Lee Stone say that they had left the air to prevent possible damage to the aerial system. He also told listeners about all the men working hard on deck the Communicator to strengthen the aerial system. Next he played the Average White Band with 'Picking up the pieces'. We were often mystified with songs giving cryptic messages about what had happened. Maybe parts had broken from the mast? We heard more about it, later that evening, when Charlie told us that we would learn the truth.

"This is the Seawolf, coming up in just a little while: the true story as to where we went for the last two days. The valiant story of the men, the ship and the antenna system that brought them all together. I'll have the true facts as soon as I concoct them. I mean, get all the facts together. OK, here it is. Get your tape recorders going. If you work for the 'Sun', obviously you want to get the true facts, if you worked for the 'Standard', especially if you're Jonathan Ashby from the 'Standard' and you're listening and want the true facts where we were for the last couple of days, get your notebook out because this is the truth, this is how she actually happened. The Men! The Ship! The Antenna system! The Waves! All that was involved. Yes. It's really quite a story. I mean, it even has love-scenes and the whole thing. I mean we concoct a story; we could tell you a lie that was made up by a PR person in New York about like, you know, that there was heavy weather and we had equipment malfunction and like antenna came down or something like that. But that is all lies. That is not what happened. Here is the truth from the words of the Seawolf."

"Now please; that's not the amazing part yet; here it is: Sea Monsters! That's right! I had the body of a giant squid and the head of an accountant and green spots on it and it was the most amazing night I ever have seen in my life, and it overtook the ship. It took Jessie Brandon hostage. I mean – I think it had a crush on Jessie, really! It took Jessie hostage and finally from Tasmania, the Tasmanian Royal Navy came to rescue and there were torpedoes and bombs, and machine-gunfire and we had actually had the whole thing on tape and this is basically what it sounded like...Yes! There they go, not Tasmanian but there goes the Monster!"

"Oh, it was a dreadful night, you should have been here. That is the true story, by the way, you may call up your friends to tell that story. But don't worry, no more sea-monsters out here, just seawolves, and all is back under control. And, oh, by the way, we got Jessie back at half price, that's the most amazing part of it. I don't think we're going away again as we were reconstructing the antenna, I mean as we were fighting off the sea-monsters there, that serpent with the Tasmanian Royal Navy, there was this rainbow amazing to see. And the sea serpent was like the former president Gerald Ford having a last meal. This is all Europe Radio, Laser 558, we're back on the air – hope you missed us!"

Well Laser was back on the air after some stressful days and certainly the Seawolf was back. If you reread the above transcript of just one segment of his program you surely understand that he really was a deejay to fool around with the listeners and journalists. What happened more, during the last week of November 1984?

Probably people on the Communicator had given all their strength during the past days as on the 26th we heard non-stop music after 9 o'clock, which lasted for almost half an hour. The reason was that Holly Michaels overslept. Also that day, between 17.00 and 21.00 BST it was the very last show on Laser 558 presented by Jessie Brandon as she got a wonderful offer to work for Capital Radio, at that time the biggest commercial station in Great Britain. Strange, looking back at the station after more than a quarter of a century is that it seems to me Jessie was far longer working on '558'. After she had left the station went back to five hour shifts with Tommy Rivers, Charlie, Holly Michaels and David Lee Stone.

Tenders came mostly from British as well as from Belgium and French ports, but came there ever a tender from Spain, which was mentioned so often to the press? Tommy Rivers remembers: "We actually had one Spanish tender, the Puntatorre, which came out in the autumn of 1984. I have pictures of this boat coming alongside and Lindau was crazy for me to get these pictures back to New York to show that we were being tendered from Spain. It was a big ocean going tug and to keep the smell down, they put ammonia on the meat and there were some dire, dire food stores on that food run. There were some things we could eat but a lot of that stuff ended over the side. We took on a hell of a lot of fuel and water also on that particular run. That was our one Spanish tender! Next to that tenders came from various little inlets and a number of people would be operating these boats and the boats changed. Sometimes they were barges; sometimes they were tug-boats. Sometimes they were coasters and even inflatables were used for small food runs. We even came out in fishing boats so every means conceivable we would be getting supplies and ferrying people."

For Monitor Magazine Martin Rosen did a farewell interview with Jessie and here just some comments from Jessie late 1984: "It depended on the season if I liked it on the Communicator. You could always tell those due for shore leave; they had the shortest tempers and were the craziest in everything. When we were coming back from shore leave on to the ship, generally things were fun. Summer was really nice, that was when the captain allowed us to visit Caroline again, despite Roy Lindau's objections. We just decided to keep it quiet, and then we were able to get back and forth; have parties. We had them over for a barbeque; they had us over for Easter and their birthday. That was fun. "

And regarding the Customs she has also a memory: "I was involved in a situation, when immigration people searched a ship I was on. I just didn't open my mouth, so they thought I was British and the captain said I was his girlfriend. They found my luggage and they said: "You know what we here for?" And I didn't dare say anything, because they would hear my American accent, so I just shook my head. He said they had a tip there were illegal immigrants. I looked alarmed. We had always radio contact when a tender came out and when we were due for shore leave, which depended on the weather, if it could tie up or not. It came from Spain of course. However, there's not one stamp from Spain in my passport!"

About using the ship's radio to call home Jessie told: "We were supposed to use it. We were told when we were hired that we would get one free phone call a month on the satellite but the only one we ever got was with Christmas. Occasionally, if there was a health problem, people were allowed to call."

And about leaving Laser: "I was going to stay on for six more months as a matter of fact, but they made me an offer, not Capital's offer. Laser made me a counter-offer and I didn't think it showed any confidence after working a year for them. I didn't think it showed any thanks, although those up at the top were quite good, they gave me a nice bonus, so I have nothing to say against them!"

The first remarkable thing I heard during the month of December was an advertisement for TROS Kompas, one of the weekly magazines from the Dutch Public Radio Societies. Followers of the Offshore Radio History know that the TROS became a household name from October 1966 in the Netherlands and has its roots with RTV Noordzee from the REM Island. It never became known to me why this advertisement was played. Of course, when I asked the press department of the TROS, they denied that they bought airtime on Laser 558, but other sources among their employees told me that the costs of the campaign was 11.000 Dutch guilders.

In December 2010 I asked former Veronica deejay Klaas Vaak (Tom Mulder), who also worked for a long time for the TROS, if he knew a reason for the airtime, bought from the Laser organisation. He responded that maybe it was 'a service of return'. The only thing I can guess is that in the weekly TROS Kompas magazine, Laser 558 was promoted for free and so the TROS Kompas commercial appeared on Laser.

December 1st brought us also Tommy Rivers who told us: ' I feel like a cowboy on the High Seas and would like to be the next presenter of the American Bandstand, as successor for Dick Clark". On the 3rd of December the transmitter went off several times with 11 minutes long during the Holly Michaels program as the longest breakdown.

We had another call from Roy Lindau who told us the results were published about the popularity of the station in Great Britain: "We're very happy as we hit the Top Three but at the moment, I can't say more. In January the figures will be published and rumours that a second station will be on our radio ship are nonsense." December 5th brought only one remark in my logging list: 'On Radio Caroline it was Bruce Purdy, who closed the station at 02.00 with: This is Radio Caroline from the MV Communicator closing down for tonight.'

The station got more international glamour when in the first week of December in the prestigious Billboard Magazine information was found about the earlier mentioned David Chaney, joining All Europe Radio Laser 558. Additional information was given: 'When living in California he worked for the Los Angeles stations KKHR, KLOS and KMET. Later on, he joined KOME based in San José'.

Laser was on the air on the 6th between 10 and 15.00 hrs BET with Holly Michaels but was suddenly replaced at 14.00 hrs by Michael Dean, but just 37 minutes later Holly was back announcing that due to technical adjustments they were going off the air. At 15.05 hrs Laser was back, this time with David Lee Stone behind the microphone. I think this was the only time that Laser 558 had three DJs within 65 minutes. I didn't hear a new slogan: 'Never be more than just over an hour away from three DJs, this is Laser 558!'

On December 7th, 1984 the result became known of the Kontiki contest. At 15.00 the names were mentioned of people who had to call within two hours to the MMI office in New York and at 20.00 four names of the winners were announced. Three winners came from England and one from the Netherlands, being Saskia Elisabeth van der Laan from Oss. Later in the evening a party was held on the MV Communicator as Captain Tim was celebrating his birthday and around 23.00 hrs it was noticeable that the alcohol was doing its work.

Some new commercials were added after the Kontiki contest was over. Bose speakers were heard again, with Selfridges as the store in Oxford Street to buy them. Later this shop was followed by PNO Audio, at Tottenham Court Road in London, just around the corner of Oxford Street. Also, Edwin Shirley Trucking and Sea Link ferries were some regulars in the programs. Another new one was 'Datalife Floppy Disks from Verbatim'. But if they brought a lot of money in it was never known.

December the 8th brought the publication of the first official survey about Laser's listenership and appeared in 'Music Week' under the headline: 'Laser claims 5 million audience in the UK'. Nearly five million listeners to Laser 558, based on the results of the MRIB radio ratings survey. 'This shows that 11 percent of the population aged 15 over had listened to the US-run station in October. The results were released by Music Media International. This is the station's advertising representative in New York.' The survey also revealed that 18 percent of the sample was aware of Laser's existence, 9 percent had listened during the previous week and 7 percent during the previous day.'

Of course, a comment was given by Roy Lindau in New York: 'I'm very pleased with Laser's ratings success in the UK. The findings of the survey are incredible when you consider that Laser has never been promoted or advertised in any medium but his own airtime. A regional breakdown of the national of average 9 percent weekly listeners shows the figure to be as high as 23 percent in the East and 14 percent in London. Other European results will be available later in the year.' Like in the sixties enormous amounts of listeners were claimed, without stating if these were on daily or weekly basis.

On Sunday the 9th, halfway through the late night show, Charlie Wolf was replaced by David Chaney as Charlie was suffering from fever, so Chaney was back on board the Communicator, and the other David (Lee Stone) went for shore leave. On the 10th Chaney was also heard during daytime hours and he brought with him a tape on which he had recorded telephone calls with the winners of the Kontiki Contest.

Around December 10th it became known that a third offshore radio station would start soon. Radio Monique would aim at Dutch and Flemish listeners, transmitting from the MV Ross Revenge and so became a sister station for Radio Caroline. They heard the news on the Communicator and on December 13th we heard for the first time a jingle: 'Laser, your hot station for Holland and Belgium.'

During the dark hours of the morning a tender came alongside on December 17th, which gave some changes in programming: 05.00 – 09.00 Ric Harris, 09.00 – 13.00 Holly Michaels, 13.00 – 17.00 Tommy Rivers, 17.00 – 21.00 David Chaney and 21.00 – 01.00 Charlie Wolf. The same Monday in the news programme on Dutch Radio 1 Member of Parliament Aad Kosto told that he would ask questions to the government about the commercials played on Laser 558 for

Public Broadcaster TROS. Also, he would ask for legal action against the Radio Monique organisation, which was breaking the law.

The Daily Mail brought on the 17th a long article about the problems within the Independent Local Radio, especially in Kent where Invicta Sound and Essex Radio really had problems to get advertisers as Laser took more and more original listeners away from them. From the New York office we heard that they received a copy of transcript from a cassette recording in which there was a talk between Eddie Blackwell from Essex Radio and Paul Rusling, earlier involved in the Laser project. In the talk between those two, one of the subjects was to hire a few people to go to the Communicator to steal some vital parts and to cut the anchor chain. Even it was suggested to bring the ship into national waters of Britain so the British authorities could act and tow the ship into a harbour, whereby the competitor for the ILR stations was a thing of the past. Both people involved in the talks denied that they spoke about the subject. In the meantime, Laser had hired a solicitor to see if legal action could be taken. Not long afterwards a copy of the transcript was received at the Freewave Media Magazine, where both Tom de Munck as well as Hans Knot were working.

During the research period for this book, I was in contact with Paul Rusling about some of the aspects of the Laser story. He disclosed to me the following story about the contacts with Eddie Blackwell and other people within the ILR stations in those days:

"There was talk about an 'anti Laser 'plot'. What happened was, I spoke often with many Laser staff who said they were not getting paid. We thought we would go and 'take over' the Communicator remove Roy Lindau and then just carry on with a different office address and some real advertising. I went too far and tried to get the funding for this 'takeover' from the ILR stations who were annoyed at Laser. Essex, Invicta and Capital were all involved."

"The actual 'plan' was simply to get the ILR stations to pay the money and use that to pay the Laser staff all the money they were owed. Enough of them were on our side for us to do a neat 'bloodless coup' and out the New York team. Laser 558 would close, to be replaced the next day by another station and a new name. We had two adverts ready to go (one of whom Lindau had pissed off with his lying) and some good support from the music industry for what we planned.

Using ILR money to affect the plan wasn't really cheating, because we would have met their requirement and removed 'Laser 558' from the air, even if it was replaced by another station. Is that really double dealing or just playing smart? "

"Eddie Blackwell was also being very subversive and recording the conversation - but he made a huge mistake. He had asked two of the Essex Radio engineers to bug the meeting for him, not realising that they were both very involved in offshore radio. One was Andy Anderson, who had designed the antenna! They were not loyal to Essex Radio at all, but they edited the tape before sending it on to Lindau. He edited it further, to suit his own dubious agenda, and sent copies to some media folk. Interestingly, no less than four people sent me a copy asking for my comments, including Thames TV where I was able to do some damage limitation and turn the 'plot' story into a plug for my book. I even showed them the Kent wharf where we planned sailing from and we filmed some of the story there."

"Unfortunately, the leak to the press scared off any chance of the ILR funding. They were worried about how it could be laundered out anyway and didn't even have a way to get funds out - the IBA closely monitored all aspects of ILR activity in those days, even asking for accounts! Without money, and with the story leaked to the press too early, we couldn't' go ahead, so Laser stumbled on for a few more months."

Paul Rusling already mentioned that letters were sent out to the press from the New York office about his book. And after reading this letter you can see that Roy Lindau wasn't happy at all with the publication. Here is the text Lindau sent to the Editorial Staff of the Freewave Media Magazine: 'I assume by now that Paul Rusling has sent a copy of his book about Laser in the hope you would write more about it. His writings are not very honest and rather inaccurate. If I remained silent it would give the book an air of authenticity. Laser 558 is successful today because of the efforts of a great team of workers. While some people have left the project, the overall turnover in personnel is lower than most land based radio stations. The real facts documented by file drawers of memos and letters in my office would make even duller reading than Paul's book.

Deka Overseas, the original investor group, engaged Paul as an engineering consultant to oversee installation of transmitters and studio equipment on the MV Communicator. After equipment was installed, he was involved with other phases of the operation like supply and programming. When he returned to England, he recruited British people to help with the project while we tried to keep it 100% American.

The balloon aerial system failed, but everyone had agreed it was an experiment worth trying. Paul had promised that if it did fail, he could rig a 'T' antenna system between the existing masts and have it operating at 45% of efficiency of the balloon aerial – all in a matter of hours. But after two weeks of trial and error trying to defeat the laws of physics, he was only able to put on a low power signal that was unmarketable as a Pan European medium. After Rusling left, a new group. Eurad SA, with 100% American crew and deejays, successfully launched Laser 558.

From his book and reports to the press in the past few months he's certainly not shown himself to be a friend of Laser. He obviously takes great pleasure in trying to bring down Laser and people he recruited into the project. As a journalist he's a good publican: his book is like an account of a stable boy taking all the credit for a Derby winner. Best Regards, Roy Lindau, President MMI.'

Of course, I asked early 2011, after more than 25 years, Paul Rusling, to comment on the contents of Roy Lindau's letter to us and he reflected with: 'My text in my book is 100% accurate, and I don't know of anyone who has ever found any inaccuracy on my pages. It is also honest, but I do omit some things - it is incomplete in some places, for example, I did not say the name of Philip Smyth ever in the book or to anyone at that time. This because I had promised him, that I would not mention his name. I always keep promises, and I do not shop (grass up / snitch) friends or clients. I also preserved my own position - because I suddenly stopped being Paul Rusling and took the alias or pseudonym of Yorkie, for many chapters in the book.

Everyone can see that, but the police could not present the book to a court as evidence that I was breaking the 1967 Marine Offences Act. My lawyer checked the text carefully to protect me, and this is another reason I know its 100% accurate, because they checked so many things. Deka Overseas was not the original group of investors, it had only one shareholder showing, then three more additional ones (all British) who Philip Smyth gave shares to. No other people put cash into the company except the original owner Philip Smyth.

It was John Kenning who approached me first and recruited me to work for a project being set up by him for his friend, Philip Smyth. I was recommended to them by the trade newspaper Broadcast. I took John Kenning to meet with Roy Lindau in New York, and later I recruited Roy Lindau to the project. He said he only joined because I was involved and he knew from Ronan that I was trustworthy and a good engineer! Ronan told me later however, that he did not tell him that, although Roy Lindau wrote this fact to me in a letter, which was dated 4th April 1983. I left the project a few weeks later, because money was not being paid to me, as was promised."

"Over the next few months, the name Laser was adopted, the frequency 729 was chosen and the balloon antenna was chosen - all done, I understand, by Roy Lindau, during June 1983, when I was not involved in the project. The project's minutes show this also. Roy Lindau removed John Kenning, over some money arguments, I think in June 1983."

At that time, Lindau recruited Paul Hodge, another ex-Caroline executive, who he worked with at Radio Caroline in 1981. It was Paul Hodge who had insisted that Paul Rusling had to come back on the project. Paul Hodge visit him at his Punch Tavern in Whitstable, paid all the project's old debts and hired him again on August 7th (1983). The next Saturday the two Pauls went to Great Yarmouth to make the payment on the ship and sent it off to Port Everglades.

"The people on board the MV Communicator for the 729 tests were all engineers, Blake Williams, Robin Adcroft (also known as Robin Banks), Dave Black-Davison, Joe Vogel and I,' remembers Rusling. "The only fires were a lot of sparks in the sky - from high voltage in the damp air and no equipment was damaged at all. We did obtain much bigger capacitors and sent the bill to Roy Lindau for payment, because he omitted them from the ship just before we sailed - that cost us the lost time and limited us to low power. I had a friend on board the ship who was a senior antenna engineer from Marconi at Chelmsford, and if it was possible to put Laser on high power with the poor and limited equipment we had, then he would have accomplished it."

"Roy Lindau often talked about investors, plural, but there was only ever one single investor. I can understand this if it was to protect Philip Smyth, but no new investors were being brought in at all. Later, a well-known UK music entrepreneur, did invest over £200,000 in cash! I understand some of this was stolen from the company, and it is odd but Roy Lindau did leave the company a few weeks later. But I was not there and do not know exactly what happened, but that investor told me personally he paid the money over in cash, and two of Roy's colleagues in Laser at that time have assured me it did not get into the company. We can only guess where it went."

"The change of company name from DEKA to EURAD SA was because the owner had given shareholdings in the original company to a couple of key people: the two guys with the first name 'Paul' for example, and Roy Lindau as well, and the owner now wanted to change that. I think my only mistake was to trust Roy's word that he would deliver, which he didn't. He cancelled equipment, he chose a balloon antenna, not me, but we know it could have worked if he did not cut out some key components, and the standby masts for the T antenna, which he also cancelled. And later, he put the blame for all his marketing decisions onto the people who had gone, experts Kenning, Hodge, Rusling, Blake Williams, Joe Vogel, etc."

"I have never snitched (grassed) on anyone. Some of the people in offshore radio, you know Hans, use violent methods and you would never dare to snitch on them. You would soon be wearing concrete boots and sat on the seabed! I think you can understand a lot by looking at the continuing friendship I have with many Laser staff, and Caroline staff from those days, and then look very hard to find any friends for Roy Lindau in the UK, in radio, in US radio sales, maybe even in his hometown" asks Paul Rusling.

On December 18th, 1984 I went into the shop for my Saturday's newspapers and so I also bought a copy of the Sun. A special was published about all kind of popular things within the music industry and so a list of the most popular Radio programs was mentioned too. On place 1: The BBC Top 40, 2 Mike Read Show and on place number 6: a complete radio station 'Laser 558'.

In the week before Christmas several drop-ins started, which were recorded by artists, wishing the listeners all best wishes for the Christmas Season. Thompson Twins, Huey Lewis, Meatloaf were just a few heard on Laser 558 where, on December 21st was the birthday for Tommy Rivers as well as more contest winners: a new air route opened between London Gatwick and Maastricht and two listeners won return tickets on Virgin Airlines to fly to the Netherlands.

Laser shortened its broadcasting hours from December 22nd due to a fuel shortage. This meant that Laser 558 was only on the air between 07.00 and 23.00 hrs BST instead of their normal 20 hours a day.

Christmas was celebrated on air with the listeners. All on board got a gift from the MMI Office in New York, a tour jacket with the Laser logo. Dinner was also good, as was mentioned a few times on the air, including a 35 pound turkey. Christmas Day was brought to a close with 'Jingle Bells' sung by the 'Communicator Tabernacle Choir'. The schedule for December 25th and 26th was: 07.00-11.00 Ric Harris, 11.00-14.00 Holly Michaels, 14.00-17.00 Tommy Rivers, 17.00-20.00 David Chaney and 20.00-23.00 Charlie Wolf, followed by an early closedown. The reason was a visit to Caroline's Ross Revenge on the 25th for sharing drinks and on the 26th some of the Caroline people came to celebrate on the Communicator.

A new commercial was heard on Christmas Day advertising Edwin Shirley Trucking, a company specialised in transporting pop groups. Another free spot we heard was for the regional rescue brigade and listeners were asked to donate money for them. December 27th it was David Chaney presenting Charlie Wolf's hours, so everyone tuning in for Charlie thought he was on shore leave. On the 27th also a tender arrived with fuel and normal '20 hours programming' restarted to bring the station into the New Year of 1985.

Jessie Brandon on the Air

Chapter 10

ANOTHER YEAR

After the Christmas bells stopped ringing, there was just another thing to celebrate. Onboard the MV Communicator they really made a party out of the New Years' celebration by doing it three times. First, they celebrated it at 23.00 hrs BET, when it became 1985 in the countries on the West continent of Europe, followed at midnight with wishes for all those listeners in Great Britain. After that they had to wait for five hours to celebrate the New Year for a third time as at that moment the Eastern Seaboard of the United States also broke into the New Year.

It was unique that the station was on the air at that time, as normally it was silent between 01.00 and 05.00 BST. During the night programmes were co-presented by Tommy Rivers, Charlie Wolf and David Chaney. Yes, indeed Charlie 'was back'. At noon, January the 4th, it was Ric Harris, reading the news. What we didn't know at that time is that it was the final Newscast ever; it was taking too much time for those onboard to compile and read it on an hourly basis. And winter arrived almost at the same time as on January the 5th Ric Harris told listeners that the deck of the Communicator was covered with five inches of snow. On Sunday January 6th the station went off the air and for four days nothing was heard from the radio ship.

Coming back to Charlie being off the air and probably on shore, we talked to the New York Office on January 9th. Lindau said that, due to remarks about the organisation in his programs, Charlie had been sacked. Three days later, Lindau regretted his decision and Wolf was allowed back on air. Lindau also said that a few days before Christmas the staff were informed about the bad financial situation and that owner Smyth had given the project a year to succeed. After pumping so much money into Laser he had decided to look for co backers in the project. Lindau mentioned there were talks with an anonymous backer to take over the whole organisation but the price asked, was too high.

Other sources told us that there were plans by the Irish owner to reorganize the New York office, which used far too much money. Lindau was the big spender and used money for things which had nothing to do with the radio. Either the budget must be reduced or the organisation office had to be closed.

On the 10th Laser was back at 14.18 with test signal and some music from the Beatles and the Stones while Ric Harris reopened the station at 15.21 to say a few words of what happened: "After a long siesta, Laser is back with music never more than a minute away. I guess it's about time we give you a plausible explanation of why you haven't heard from Laser in the past few days and what happened. You wouldn't believe it. About three days ago, was it? A giant Albatross landed on our aerial system and got electrocuted and died there and just fouled everything up, short circuits, the whole works. And it took us three days to convince Charlie Wolf that he was the only person here to fit to climb the aerial system and clean up the mess and get the things going. He took a lot of convincing too, I'll tell you. We told him he had his choice, he could either climb the aerial, five thousands of feet or whatever it is, or he could help us test out our new personal floatation devices, which were basically pieces of angle-iron."

And later that day Charlie Wolf came with another explanation: "Well, I must tell the truth. Dennis Thatcher, good friend of mine, we're long buddies from way back when. Dennis was holding a party over the weekend and who am I to turn down an invitation to a party with Dennis Thatcher. And so, I thought I take the whole crew along. Right? So, we picked up anchor and took the Communicator up the Thames Estuary there, right up the Thames, right into London. Great party! The only problem there was we've got the big two-hundred foot masts that the antenna is on. And well, there's some bridges along the way that are kind of short and it really messed up the antenna system; and you should have seen what it did to the bridges. But a great party! Dennis, thanks a bunch, let's do it again."

Later he went on with: "I haven't been in this room for three, four days. Well, I mean, after the Dennis Thatcher party you needed several days to calm down and get back into the things of swings. The antenna system had come down in a very bad storm out here. It was horrible. Our neighbours to the north, their anchor broke; they were a quarter of a mile of us; water going over the bow. I'm not a sailor. I'm not into this waves splashing, wind blowing routine! But anyway, engineers got the antenna up, we put some Instant Karma into the system and all is just hunky-dory here!"

The next day, January 11th, David Lee Stone was back on the ship to replace David Chaney, who went on shore leave. Just a few days of normal programming followed, David Lee Stone returning to the ship and Holly Michaels leaving but on January 14th, during the Ric Harris show problems restarted. At 6.00 BET, an hour into his program, there was sudden silence as the transmitter abruptly failed. It remained silent until the 18th when at 15.00 hours the signal was back with unannounced album sides. This went on for two hours, followed by Tommy Rivers who told: "We're back on our temporary aerial". After him Dave Lee Stone took over, followed by Charlie Wolf.

Charlie once again had one of his funny stories. "Laser 558, the Seawolf here. We're back on the air, finally, again, for the 733rd time. We're trying to get our stuff together here – Wallies in the organization. No actually, what really honestly happened, as David Lee Stone has pontificated earlier, there was a hole in the ocean! Someone put a hole or put the stopper out, of the bottom of the North Sea. The whole thing drained out. We were on sand, which totally ruined the aerial system, because as you know the antenna reflects off the water. It's a whole complicated kind of thing. But we got it all filled up again, the ship is rocking about right now. Lots of waves and everyone is getting seasick and they're so happy because this is something they really missed!"

It took some time but at a later stage we learned that the blizzard, that was blowing on the morning of January the 14th, bent the top fifty feet of the Communicator's forward lattice aerial mast. It bent at a 90 degree angle towards the bow. A temporary antenna had to be rigged, which got the station back on the air on very low power. I heard from Buster Pearson in South Benfleet in Essex, not far from the Communicator, that listening during darkness hours was difficult. Worked continued at the mast and so the transmitter went off several times for maintenance.

Earlier on I mentioned that people had to live together on a ship for a longer period, without knowing each other before. How did Tommy Rivers for instance get on with the other staff on the ship?

"It was good, it varied as well and as the station evolved and we had different personalities come and go, it was all great fun and, of course, we had 50% guys and 50% gals and that was a pretty good arrangement actually! When we started, we had a marine crew of

American guys from the state of Maine. Tim Levensaler was captain and a couple of his buddies were there and over the run of the next 18 months, the marine side changed considerably. Brits are working out there as well. I guess the most memorable captain was Captain Bob Kermath, from Dundee and he was a great, older guy. He started out sailing merchant ships during World War II. He'd been on boats that had gone down twice. He had some great tales from the sea and he'd been all over the world on cargo vessels and was getting into his retirement years. He had time for a boat that was going nowhere, where most guys of that ilk wouldn't put up with that sort of thing."

In the meantime, Laser appeared in the newspapers and magazines again as on January 18th 'Broadcast' brought the header: 'Radio Laser Hits Sales Warning'. 'The future for Radio Laser looks bleak with the news that the station's home, the MV Communicator, is up for sale. Millionaire Richard Branson is said to be among those interested in buying the ship. It has been offered for sale by the owners, Eurad SA. But it is believed that three parties have been in touch with Philip Smyth, the Dublin hotelier, named in London's Standard on August 30th, 1984 as Laser's principal backer, with a view to purchasing the ship and operating a radio station aboard. One interested party is headed by Chris Cary, the ex-Radio Luxembourg deejay and owner of the hugely successful Irish Station Radio Nova. He has a long involvement in potential offshore radio projects and the interest has been heightened with the arrival of Q102, a new competitor for his Nova operation in Dublin. Another interested consortium is said to be headed by Richard Branson, the boss of Virgin Records and Virgin Airways. He too has an interest in offshore radio projects and 18 months ago sought a controlling interest in the relaunch of Radio Caroline. If Branson were to conclude a deal with the Laser organisation it is unclear how the IBA would view an ILR investor operating a station that is widely regarded as the greatest threat to profitability of a number of ILR stations in the south and the east of England. The third interested party is based in East Anglia and includes several ex offshore radio broadcasters. If any of these three parties were to purchase the Communicator it is likely the station would depart from its all American DJ line-up although it is very successful 'all-hit-radio' format would remain."

On the 18th morale was bad on the ship, low power and no supplies elicited some comments. Ric Harris announced that they were listening to 'local Radio 33 1/3'. It must have been a big experience for the Yankees to be on the Communicator. The signal was so bad that I couldn't receive a thing in Groningen. The next afternoon we had an early call with MMI office in New York. Six hours' time difference and so Lindau just came into the office to tell us that the financial backer Smyth gave the office just 60 more days to bring things into good financial order. He added that Smyth also mentioned to put the whole thing up for sale if they wouldn't succeed. Just two days later a small article in the 'Daily Mail' suggested that: 'Pop pirate may be sunk by cash crises., as the station had failed to find enough international advertising. 'The next two months are said to be crucial. Storm damage has forced Laser off the air twice in three weeks.'

Talking about low supplies it must have been frustrating for those on the MV Communicator. But did they have a proper cook aboard the vessel? A question that was asked by Chris Edwards; Tommy Rivers remembered: "Sometimes we did it our self but most of the time we had somebody out there to cook. We had a guy from Kansas called Michael Dean who used to cook and walk in on some of the shows and talk about recipes etc. We also had a guy from Lisbon, Portugal, Martine, who made the best Portuguese omelette in the world, it was fantastic. I had to have one every morning with a can of Dr. Pepper. It was a weird experience but we would stay up until two or three in the morning watching videos etc. and wake up at the break of noon and get ready for your show.

For the remaining days of January 1985, the station was almost daily off the air for various reasons and varying periods of time. Laser was starting on the 22nd, when David Lee Stone told us at 16.00 hrs that the station would close down, as work had to be done on the aerial as well as in the studio. David told the listeners that they would be back the same evening. We tuned in a few times, but it was no earlier than around 21.20 on the 23rd that Laser was on 558 kHz again.

On January 23rd we were informed by the New York office that Roy Lindau had been dismissed as President of Music Media International and that he would be replaced by John Moss.

Time to go to the John Catlett interview which Chris Edwards had with him in August 1987 and Chris asked him: 'Where did John Moss fit into all this? John answered with: 'John Moss was hired as a salesman in the winter of 1984-1985 and was quite successful in selling advertising. When Roy Lindau left the company, John Moss became the president of Music Media International, which was the sales operation behind Laser 558.'

Luckily enough we heard normal programming from Laser 558 from 6.30 till closedown on January 24th, 1985. The same day the Magazine 'Marketing' headed: 'Lindau deserts Laser'. The story told us that in the midst of rumours about Radio Laser's possible sale, Roy Lindau had resigned as President of Music Media International, the New York agency which marketed the North Sea's station airtime. John Moss, formerly vice-president, took the place of president of MMI when Lindau left. The article went on with: 'Since September the station had run a sprinkling of American-sourced adds, but so far revenue has failed to meet running costs of $3000 a day. Ironically, the station was scheduled to break even for the first time next month, when it is expected to take $ 100.000. But the recent spate of icy weather and choppy sea could have scuppered that. It needs to be broadcasting without interruption throughout the whole month of February to take the full $ 100.000. Over the recent weeks there has been speculation that Laser is up for sale.'

John Moss denied to the journalist of 'Marketing' that the station was to be sold but admitted that Laser's lawyers had discussions with the earlier mentioned Branson and Cary: "We're are after all in the business to make money, so we do follow up enquiries. But people from all over the planet approach us all the time. We are not currently seeking suitors for Laser."

Meanwhile back on the ship some cartridges were filled with new commercials for a record by Don Henley: 'The boys of summer' (played during winter) and for a movie – which would become a massive success - Beverly Hill Cops. They did inform the listener in time about a breakdown in transmission, which was also happening on the 25th. At 10.00 o'clock in the morning it was Ric Harris announcing that the station would close down for aerial maintenance and that there would be silenced for the main part of the day. He couldn't tell when but was sure there would be a different Laser in the future: "When we come back there is one thing for sure, the signal will be stronger, louder, brighter, cleaner, clearer and better than ever before." A pity they didn't realize the promised upgrading as in the afternoon, around 16.45 Michael Dean could be heard, but the power increase was not materialised. Normal programming went on till close down at 01.00. Next day started with Ric Harris, who closed his program at 9.56 – it was already Saturday 26th. With the message that they would be off the air for the remaining day hours but just 15 minutes later they were back on the air. Weather conditions were probably the reason they couldn't work on deck.

The next day it was announced by the office that plans to bring the weekly syndicate programme 'American Top 40' presented by Casey Kasem, had stopped. This due to the fact that the syndicator ABC Watermark now didn't want to have any contacts with pirates!

On January 27th there were two small interruptions in programming while on the 28th the day was started with an hour non-stop, followed by Ric Harris and his colleagues. Just a small break in the late afternoon followed and problems with Charlie Wolf's stomach and so Tommy Rivers and 'Stoner' which was the nickname of David Lee Stone, took over till closedown that night.

The following day they went off-air at 3pm for yet more aerial work and returned two hours later, still on low power. Not everybody was happy with the work as Charlie suggested in his program that it could take up to a fortnight before work was totally done. On January 30th they started up with an hour late and a closed down at 08.00 hrs when Ric Harris, again promised a much better signal. Apart from a brief carrier, the station was silent.

Bigger, better and louder than before could be said from the last day of January when Laser returned loud and clear, starting at 5.00 o'clock with a five hours show featuring Ric Harris. Tommy Rivers and Dave Lee Stone also did as five hours stints until Charlie Wolf took over at 20.00 hrs. However, after 44 minutes into his show there was suddenly dead air. After a minute Ric Harris and Michael Dean came into the studio and told the listeners that Charlie was having a nervous breakdown, so Michael took over the program. Buster Pearson mentioned the next day that a more likely explanation of Charlie's indisposition was that he had been bitten by the ship's dog, Clever Trevor. In fact, a couple of days later he told us on air that this had been the case.

Buster, as an attentive listener, observed that since the return to high power the music had a tendency to run slightly too slow. This was particularly noticeable during Michael's short visit to the microphone; the slowing phenomenon accelerated markedly until the transmitter abruptly cut at 22.03 BST. It stayed silence for seven minutes when the station was back with Charlie, having made a remarkable recovery, mike-side; and he then proceeded to present one of the most hilarious programs we've ever heard from him.

Here is the full transcript which was written down at 31 Avondale Road in South Benfleet: "Seawolf had a few words to say about their return from 'All Sheppey Radio': "It's so good to get into Holland and Germany – I've got friends in Germany right now, the fighting 128th Public Affairs Detachment of the Utah National Guard. They are in Germany right now on manoeuvres of some sort of 'hello' to them... OK you've an itch for a 'fever pitch', right? OK, let us do it! Let us go forth into fever pitch land! Do that funky thing. Remember, on restrictive clothing, please. Oxygen throughout the room, for your convenience. We are getting out, out and about, because our antenna has been fixed. And it's amazing how we did it. I will just quickly recap what has happened. Two weeks ago, big storm: real, I mean, how big...oooooh – that big! Yes, big enough to make people go 'Oooh, aah, and it knocked our forward mast right in half. It's a two hundred foot bean-pole and it just split it right in half, It was a mess, it really was."

"And we had a temporary mast up...and it was cock-eyed. It really was. So, we have been working on it and trying to fix it. And believe it or not we came up with a marvellous solution! This is something that defied science! I told them what happened, the antenna system broke down. Why don't you tell them we got back to where we got now, the massive coverage area, the good signal?" David Lee Stone was in the studio to add: "The thing is, we had to brave the worst weather imaginable, high winds, rain, sleet – everything but snow. I mean like hurricane force winds. We had to climb up the mast and we had to literally take down the old, bent up, wrecked twisted pieces of wreckage and replace them with new tower sections. It's a good thing we had the tower sections on hand you see. We had plenty of those, you know, left over. We already had them onboard and that was the saving grace as we already had them, because otherwise we would have taken forever to get them from Spain".

Next Charlie interjected by telling us that it was all lies: "Folks, let us be reasonable here, C'mon it's you and me talking here, OK? What do you do, you're driving along, right? And you hit a low tree and your aerial on your car breaks, what do you do? How do you fix it? Coat hanger! A wire coat hanger! We didn't do anything with a tower or an aerial. We got the largest coat hanger because she wore big coats, OK? So, we took this giant, a hundred and fifty foot coat hanger, we undid it ...": David just couldn't take this and added: "Charlie, what are you talking about? You are asking for trouble I can't believe it."

Sea Wolf: "I've got to give them the truth. It's a coat hanger on the front deck. Come on out some time, it's there; look at the thing, would I lie to you? I mean, who are you going to believe? Him? C'mon, he's a poser." "Charlie, you've got to be kidding! I don't believe you." Charlie came back with: "I had to tell them the truth, David."

"A coat hanger? No one is going to believe that."

"Well, it's the truth", insisted Charlie, "And I know you're going to try and lie your way out of it because you're always trying to show me up!" Well, the new aerial was there, with two deejays fighting for their own truth as well. January 1985 came to an end for Laser 558 with high power and maybe more listeners.

Charlie Wolf

Chapter 11

WAS FEBRUARY 1985 BETTER?

We asked ourselves, after the disasters in the month before, if February 1985 would bring us more fun with Laser 558. The first indication of the positive determination to continue came from comments in 'Music Week' dated the 2nd: 'Laser 558 is denying reports that it is to disappear and that its home, the MV Communicator, is up for sale for 1.5 million pounds. The article claimed that the rumours have been compounded by technical problems aboard the ship. "We are not for sale and are not going off the air", says Jane Morris, spokeswoman for Music Media International. Of the technical difficulties Morris says: "the top four sections of the back mast holding the antenna snapped off in the bad weather, which meant the signal was not being broadcast at full power. We went out at about half power, occasionally going off the air. This led to complaints of spotty reception, and not being able to pick us up at night."

The article said that repairs which will add an extra 10 feet to the 100 feet mast were underway, which the station expected to begin broadcasts with an improvement signal this week. Morris is in the UK to announce the appointment of new Laser deejays and to further quell rumours'.

Jane Morris's information was badly at fault because it was the front mast, not the back mast, that was storm damaged. Also, on the 2nd we heard the first of a new series of commercials for a chain of clothing shops in London with the unlikely name of 'Dickie Dirts'. The first one we noted was at 9.30 in the morning and they were tied in with a mention of Levi's jeans.

The first new deejay in 1985 was heard on Sunday the 3rd of February in the 20.00 to 01.00 slot. It was Chris Carson, from Iowa. She presented her first programme with great confidence. After Jessie Brandon left the station another female presenter joined. And what had we to believe from a short article in the Daily Mirror from Monday February the 4th. John Blake wrote: 'Laser 558, the smash hits pirate radio station that is pounding away at Radio One's audience, is about to start a second radio station to compete with

Radio Two. The channel will play what the Americans call Adult Orientated Rock by groups like The Police, Genesis, Eagles and Steely Dan, says a Laser spokesman.'

Another logging came from February 8th when there was another winter storm on the North Sea. Christine, as Chris Carson called herself that day, became so seasick that, in her fourth hour of presenting that day, she had to stop and her programme was taken over by Tommy Rivers, who closed down the station at 01.00 hrs BET. When tuning in during the morning there was a breakdown for 11 minutes and at 6.38 Ric Harris was back, but not for long. At 6.48 the station went off the air not coming back before 11.40 hrs, when 20 minutes of non-stop music followed.

Tommy Rivers started regularly programming at 12.00. But for the next 24 hours the storm became stronger. February 9th brought the following line up: 05.00- 10.00 Ric Harris, 10.00-15.00 Tommy Rivers followed by David Lee Stone between 15.00 and 20.00 hrs. At the end of his show Stoner said: "I've just about had enough". The storm, according North Foreland Radio, was Easterly Force 8 and comments were being made aboard the MV Ross Revenge, the radio vessel housing Radio Caroline and Radio Monique, that they were watching their neighbours imitating a submarine.

Both ships were anchored in sight of each other. When David Lee Stone was finished, Chris Carson took over and it seemed that she was in much better condition than the previous evening. She even sounded cheerful despite the weather conditions. Her programme continued up until midnight when it was decided that due to the ferocity of the storm it was advisable to switch off the transmitter an hour earlier than normal. So, Laser 558 signed off with the usual closing theme: 'Thank you for the music' from Abba.

Would there be more music the next day? It was not a question we thought about at the moment Abba was played, but the next morning, February 10th there was no signal at all on '558'. Around lunchtime I switched my transistor on Radio Monique and not much later I learned that the MV Communicator again was into problems as they announced that the ship had lost another mast during the storm. On the 11th Buster Pearson wrote down that during the programs on Radio Caroline he heard several calls to the MV Communicator to contact the people on the Ross Revenge on channel 16. This occurred during the Dave Richards Show and at 20.44 hrs he explained that the Communicator had just dropped her reserve anchor as, in the continuing mountainous seas she had lost her main anchor. All on board were safe intending to resume the normal programming as soon as possible. Dave sent good wishes to their neighbours and added: "We know how it feels lads!"

Until February 14th Laser's signal was off the air when, around 15.30 hrs, nonstop music started. This lasted up till 16.00 hrs when David Lee Stone presented a show for two hours and at 16.22, he told us about Laser's absence during the past days:

"You know, a huge winter storm that dumped a lot of snow all over parts of England, Scotland and Wales? Well, we got hit by it pretty hard too, and our aerial came down again. It took a few days and we hope you're receiving us loud and clear, and hope to be up and running through the rest of the winter. Fingers crossed here on the MV Communicator. We think it's going to last this time, we've really got everything bolted down, tightened up and just generally all buffed out, if you know what I mean". It was the top section of the forward mast that had again collapsed; and sadly, the station had not this time returned to high power and could be heard only with difficulty during darkness. "

Liz West, Charlie Wolf and Erin Kelly

Ric Harris was replaced by a woman; David Lee Stone announced at 16.51 that a new girl DJ would be on the air that night, called Liz West. This turned out to be somewhat premature as Tommy Rivers was followed at 20.00 hrs by Chris Carson who led us to the clock of 22.00 hrs. Then, to our surprise, yet another new female DJ appeared on Laser 558. It was Erin Kelly, who was presenting the only three hour programme that night. One hour in her programme she confessed that the past hour was the longest ever in her life and that she had been continuously vomiting into a bucket; the violent February storm went on to rage outside. Erin came from Alabama and she told the listeners that her hometown made a name of fame when the Rolling Stones recorded their hit 'Brown Sugar' there.

On the 15th the station had a late start as only at 6.45 hrs Tommy Rivers was back in the hot seat till 9.00 when Erin Kelly followed till 13.00 hrs. David Lee Stone could be heard for the next four hours leading us into the 17 till 21 hrs spot with Chris Carson. She was followed till closedown time at 01.00 hrs by Liz West, who presented her first programme on Laser 558. Liz informed her listeners that she came from Florida and her first programme was handled extremely competently. Well at least there were again 5 deejays on the ship which brought us back to four hours slots. Another remarkable moment for the history of Offshore Radio as February the 15th 1985 went into the books as the first day ever the girls outnumbered the boys on one radio station, transmitting from International Waters.

In an interview with Liz West, which was published in OEM, Liz was asked what made her decide to come from the US to England she answered: "A multitude of things really. I've always been one for challenges. I am an adventure seeker and, like most people, I have always liked to go to Europe. With this job I got 13 weeks a year holiday and 13 weeks to see Europe has got to be a perk."

On the question why she thought Laser was so successful she answered: "It's the music, not to be overly judgemental of media here, there is a very small media pool here. It's a large area with a very small media pool to draw from. People do not have a lot of choice and because of the needle laws over here a person will only get on an average, from a government regulated station, a very small amount of music per hour, the best being meaningful chatter! You could find yourself tuning into a radio station hearing Bryan Adams followed by a 45 minutes long discussion on the joys of asparagus.

People can tune into Laser, getting a minimal amount of chatter. When we do open our mouths, we have something to say. It's usually something exciting hopefully, without the hype. We are Americans so there is a dash of novelty there and we play all the hits – we play proven chartered hits all day."

Chris Edwards of OEM also asked Tommy Rivers in an interview how they did get on with the people on board the MV Ross Revenge, anchored not far away and in sight of the MV Communicator: "We got on great with those guys. I know that Ronan and Lindau didn't want us to talk to each other but we leaned on each other and we used to go back and forth and visit each other. If we ran out of things, we ran over there in the inflatable boat and vice versa. When we broke anchor chains, we'd call each other up and get ourselves back to position. We got on really well out there. People like Johnny Lewis, whom I'm still in touch with, Stewart Vincent and the rest. It was good times out there."

Charlie Wolf was asked to do some words for a new press report from the office at Music Media International in New York: 'Liz, Chris and Erin are a welcome addition to the all American male air staff now heard on Laser which includes: Program Director David Lee Stone and air talent Charlie Wolf, Ric Harris and Tommy Rivers. Although the three new deejays hail from different parts of the USA, they all welcome the adventure of broadcasting to a large Pan- European audience from the North Sea.'

John Moss, President of MMI commented: 'Liz, Chris and Erin offer a vitality and energy that our audience will clearly delight in. Their voices and presentation are extremely high calibre and we are proud they've chosen Laser as a platform for their talent. Our listeners are going to love them.'

Liz West joined Laser from Palm Spring in California. Her radio background included postings at WDIZ Orlando Florida and 98 Rock in Tampa Florida. Her favourite bands at the time included Gentle Giant and Blanc Mange and she was 24 years of age when getting aboard the MV Communicator. Erin Kelly had been on the radio in the United States for nine years before deciding to make the big jump to the North Sea. She joined Laser 558 from WVNA in Muscle Shoals, Alabama, where she was doing the early morning show.

Erin was 23 years of age when coming to Europe and her favourites at the time were Talking Heads, Psychedelic Furs and David Bowie. She was also a professional photographer, played the guitar and loved writing poems. Going to a pirate station was no problem to her as she was holding a green belt in karate and was planning to continue the discipline aboard the Communicator. Finally, something about Chris Carson, who joined from Iowa City, where she worked for four years in radio and was on KKRQ before signing a contract with MMI. Her favourites at the time were Duran, Duran, Prince and Frankie Goes to Hollywood. Surprisingly, she spoke not only English but also fluently Dutch and French.

Going back to the loggings we've to mention that no signal was heard at my place in Groningen and the signal was barely audible throughout the day and the evening in Benfleet, which was 20 miles away from the anchorage from the Laser radio ship. The next day the signal was a bit improved, but the station was still broadcasting on very low power. Next day, it was Monday the 18th, saw a resumption of the Communicator Club Lucky Numbers game and the first two winners were heard at 8.35 in the morning. It was a number belonging to someone in Matlock as well as to a person in Dunstable. Once again it was the rule that someone who heard a mentioning of his lucky number had to send a postcard to the MMI address in New York to receive his Laser Album package.

The same day a large article appeared in 'The Guardian', which brought the first interview with John Moss to be published in Great Britain after he became the new President of Music Media International. Some of the things he had to say were: "The advertising business is coming to us from the UK and is all placed in the USA and no sales are made in Great Britain. That is not a lack of interest. We are receiving ten inquires a week and we spend a lot of time turning them away and we say: "Support your local radio station". In fact, if ILR (Independent Local Radio) wanted us to promote their advertising medium, I'd be prepared to do it. If ILR is healthy, that's good to everybody.' John Moss had also some remarks about the copyright fees: 'we have offered to pay the record companies and we have offered not to play their discs. They don't want it either. And the performers are not beating us up the way the regulatory bodies say they are – we make them popular!'

Some newspapers wrote about interference that Laser could have made, and John Moss reflected with: 'We're professional broadcasters; we've got very modern equipment, we produce a very clear signal and it doesn't wander off 558 metres (sic) medium wave. Once, when there was a big Irish sport event, RTE claimed that they were worried. So, we closed down a while during the commentary – and we still got a complaint. It wasn't us. This is not just dangling our antenna out of the bedroom window.'

John Moss also had something to say about the regulations within the British radio system: 'Of course that's not how radio works, it's not like television where you are only around the set at certain times of the day and need to get the mix available then. You carry the radio to the bathroom or you have it on in the car and you want to have your sort of programmes on tap at that time. Now you get an hour of jazz, or whatever, at five o'clock and nothing more if you missed it.'

John Moss also reflected on the dozens of demo-tapes the office received: 'Seventy percent of them are from women and the standard was very high. We have gone through the phase of attracting adventurers and started appealing to broadcasting talent'. The journalist from the Guardian, Peter Fiddick, added: 'The success of Jessie Brandon taught them one lesson: there will be now four women and four men on the expanded team, ferrying to and fro using a two months on, one month off rota.'

February 20th, when he closed down his show at 17.00 hrs, it was holiday time for David Lee Stone. In the evening of the same day several calls were put out to the MV Communicator over the airwaves from Radio Caroline, The Coastguards were apparently experiencing some difficulty in contacting people at the home of Laser 558 and had asked people on the Ross Revenge to relay the message to their colleagues on the Communicator. When the message eventually reached those on the Laser ship the station immediately went off the airwaves for a few minutes. They returned at 21.18 hrs and it was Chris Carson who told in her program that they were always happy to assist the Coastguards. Buster Pearson suggested that apparently the Coastal Radio Services had been experiencing some interference but he added: 'But whatever it was coming from it was certainly not from the radio ships!'

Johnnie Lewis, who was back on the Ross Revenge, later recalled the rare incident: 'It was a funny one, hilarious. The Coastguard called us up. I was on the bridge and North Foreland Radio was calling us, and they said: "Do you ever have contact with the Communicator? Can you give them a call? We've a complaint, their transmissions coming over our signal on 500 kHz". So, I called them up, but they weren't answering. There was nobody on their bridge. We've got great big arc-lights on top of our bridge from when we used to be a big fishing trawler, so we kept turning them on and off to 'flash' them and after about fifteen minutes eventually they answered and we told them the problem. They called the Coastguards then, and obviously we were listening. The Coastguard said: "Can you have a check of you transmitters because we're getting interference from you?"

"They went down and checked and they said: "Well, at the moment we can't see anything wrong with the transmitters, if you like we'll turn them off and you see if the interference clears." They turned the transmitters off and the Coastguards said: "Well, it's still there;" at which point thought: 'O, Christ, it's us! So, we turned our transmitters off as well and it was still there. It turned out to be a huge great World Service transmitter and one from BBC's Radio One. It had nothing to do with Laser or Caroline."

"In all fairness to the people at North Foreland Radio they apologized and wished us the best of luck. Parkstone Quay (Harwich) came on as well, and said they've got no problems with our signal, never had and told us that if it would happen, they also should give us a call. Obviously, it was good to keep a relationship between us and the Coastguards going. We had some regular chats with them during those days and they asked us for advice. In foggy weather they asked how far we could see from the bridge of the Ross Revenge and if we could see the Long Sand beacon. The Coastguard wouldn't handle phone calls and we knew we couldn't ask them so as it was forbidden by the law. We wanted to have good relations and we didn't want to put them on the spot. We wanted to keep everything on the level. Just talking to them wasn't breaking any law and was also not causing any problem.

A day later, on the 21st of February, we saw the return of 'five hours shows', after David Lee Stone had departed. Fifteen of the twenty daily hours were then presented by the girls on the ship and they heard the word 'the Laserettes' introduced for the girls, by Erin Kelly. On the 23rd of February, a Saturday, normal programming started with Tommy Rivers from 05.00 to 09.00 and Erin Kelly took over till 10.59 when once again the station went off the air for maintenance to reduce the output power. Listeners were advised by Erin to stay tuned to '558' and at 13.39 hrs an unmodulated signal was back, still on low power. Work wasn't done completely as it took up to 13.58 to hear Erin again until 16.00. And then, after a two weeks holiday, we heard the return of Ric Harris taking over the hours between 16.00 and 19.00. Chris Carson went, up till 22.00 hrs, behind the mike, as Liz West took the hours followed, to close down time at 01.00 hrs.

When switching on the next morning we learned that Laser was off the air and it took up till 17.21 that non-stop music started, which lasted up till 17.30 when the transmitter was switched off again. This lasted for 13 minutes and at 18.00 hrs normal programming started with 2 hours shows and a special get together of almost all onboard between 23.00 and 01.00. The three girls were heard as well as Tommy Rivers and Michael Dean. Ric Harris was the only one to be silent as he was sleeping to get up early for his morning show on the next day, February 25th.

Ric came on for three hours as they wanted to do more work on the antenna system. They worked for many hours as we had to wait till 17.07 when Erin took the microphone and normal programming terminated until regular closedown time. On the 26th normal programming was heard till 13.00 hrs when more work started on deck. Silence commenced on '558' until 15.15 hrs on the 27th, when an unmodulated carrier was heard – including switching off and on several times. Music was heard for the first time at 15.35 hrs and it was a happy moment as for the first time they were on high power again. Information gained from the shows told us that repairs had been completed to the forward mast and its height raised by ten foot.

On the 28th there were test signals at 16.30 and after 20 minutes the first music was heard, being an album track from the Doors. Normal programming commenced at 17.00 with Tommy Rivers. The last day for February brought us Ric from 05.00 to 09.00, when Erin followed for a one hour show. At the end she told us that the station would be off again for some hours of maintenance. She was back on air with another one hour show, when normal programming ended that month at 01.00 hrs.

Chapter 12

EARLY MARCH ON THE TV

March 1985 started with, what was announced as a special interview with Charlie Wolf on Channel Four Television in the programme 'The Tube'. On Oracles pages, it was mentioned earlier that day that 'DJ Charlie Wolf of Laser radio fame will be chatting to Jools about the growing popularity of pirate radio stations'. However, that was one thing that wasn't discussed. In total it was a 130 seconds long interview in which Charlie thanked the listeners for all the mail coming to the ship. He also explained that the new records were delivered to the ship via the satellite link and he did try to make Jools understand that Laser was not an illegal station. But Jools gave every impression to the viewers that the station was illegal and took all the fun out of it.

On March the 1st programme changes took place. From 05.00 till 09.00 Ric Harris could be heard, followed by Erin till 13.00. Next was Tommy Rivers till 18.00. Then an hour of Ric again, as Erin Kelly took another one hour. At 20.00 hrs till midnight, we heard Christine Carson, who told that she was sitting in for Liz West, who wasn't feeling good as she had a little cold. The next day, however, Liz told another story as the reason she wasn't heard on the previous day was that she went out to the neighbours on the Ross Revenge to borrow some sugar. From the US office we heard that David Chaney left the organisation as he could get a better job in the USA. March 2nd Liz was on between 22.00 and 01.00 and during the last hour she introduced a new item, which was a one hour show with only album tracks. It did not come as a Liz West presentation as the tracks were spun by Christine Carson.

Note blocks were always on our desks and so we wrote down on March the 4th that a few new commercials were heard; the first one for Terrarium Computer Games. The spots were read out every two hours by the on air jock, which was also done with the new series of Kontiki and Virgin Airlines spots. March 4th also brought the results of listening figures in the Netherlands. 8% of Dutch inhabitants listened to offshore radio on a regular base. 59% from that group had Caroline as a favourite, 25% Radio Monique and Laser 558 reached 17% of that group. The authorities came around the corner of the

Communicator anchorage as on March the 5th we learned in the morning that a Police boat was in the vicinity of the radio ship to make photographs. And so, interaction was heard as one record was dedicated to the persons on the Police vessel. In the afternoon, at 13.00 hrs, we heard David Lee Stone again. He returned from Portugal where he was on holiday. With the tender, Stone came to the ship, it were Christine Carson and Tommy Rivers leaving to take a vacation.

Another one returning to the station was Charlie Wolf, who told that the tender arrived at 02.00 in the night and that he was very surprised to see the girls on the ship, on which he thought at first they were 'go go dancers', until they told him that they were the 'Laserettes'. As I always thought that Charlie was the one onboard the Communicator to go over the edge, that night he gave us more information about the Police vessel. He openly told the listeners that it was the MV Ian Jacobs, which had Ipswich as home harbour. He also suggested that they could let him have copies of some of the many photos they took. He then thanked them for the beer and the newspapers, and asked them to remember, the next time they came by, that he drinks milk!

On the 7th Liz needed a break and so Erin extended her show until 14.00 hrs while Stoner took the hours till 19.00; following was Charlie up till midnight. The last hour from that 'day' was presented by Michael Dean, who did one of his rare appearances. Next a step to March the 9th, as the last hour of Charlie's late evening show was announced as the 'classic tracks hour'. We heard it once before but it remained a rarity. On the 10th of March Erin Kelly was not heard and so it was back to five hour shows. Another thing to mention for that day was that at 22.41 a new spot was heard, this time for 'The Laser Music Weekend', which was to commence on the 14th of March at Calstor near Great Yarmouth. The same day the station closed down at midnight, this due to the bad weather.

March 11th authorities stopped once again a tender and arrested some people for questioning. On Tuesday the 12th there were further changes in programming. Till 15.00 hrs, and the start of Liz West's show, everything was as before. But at 16.45 hrs, when tuning in again, Charlie was on an unusual spot for him. He was on up till 21.00 hrs and then we were honoured with the presence of Mighty Joe Young, who presented only his second show during his long stay aboard the Communicator.

The last hour, till closedown, was another Michael Dean appearance on Laser 558. A new commercial was heard for a bungalow park, including a concert show with performances by Paul Young and Modern Romance. The entrance fee was 25 Pounds.

On the 13th, Ric did the early programme up till 10.00, when surprisingly Charlie Wolf took over. During his program, five minutes to Midday, Liz and Erin came in to surprise him with some Cadbury Chocolate and they also said 'hello' to John Moss, who was in London for business. A few minutes past one in the afternoon Charlie announced the station would be off the air for some hours, due to maintenance to the antenna system and immediately the transmitter was switched off. It was 16.25 hrs when non-stop music was heard, and David Lee Stone took over till 19.00 hrs when Erin Kelly followed till 22.00 hours. The last three hours for the day were filled with music by Liz West.

In Benfleet Buster Pearson wrote down that day that the signal from Laser was stronger than ever before. In fact, he logged a signal 9 and +35 dBs and he thought the station used for the first time their full power of 25 kW.

March 15th a new Press Release was send out by MMI from the New York offices: 'Music Media International, exclusive world-wide representative for Laser 558 Radio, announced today the appointment of Bradley Ughetta as International Account Executive. Bradley joins from NBC's owned and operated WRC-AM in Washington, where he was an Account Executive. He's a graduate of New York University at Oneonta with a marketing and account degree. He also served as Programme Director and General Manager of his college radio station WONY-FM. John Moss, President of Music Media International, commented a few words on the appointment: 'Brad Ughetta brings the bright combination of energy, vitality and experience to our sales staff. Hiring him was our first step in expanding our current sales effort, in order to capitalize on the advertiser acceptance Laser 558 is currently enjoying in the marketplace'.

No remarkable things happened until the 20th when Ric Harris went on shore leave and his morning programme was taken over by David Lee Stone. Also, the tender brought Chris Carson back on the MV Communicator as she was heard that day between 13.00 and 17.00

hrs. In Dutch harbour and navy place Den Helder the Radio Monique Drive Inn Show took place at the venue 'Huize Tijdverdrijf'. People visiting the show were astonished that the show had a double name as also a billboard for the Laser Road Show was showed. It was a co- presentation between Nico van der Steen (Monique) and Tommy Rivers (Laser). The next day a new commercial was heard in the late afternoon, a promo for the then new single of Maxwell Silvers: 'Seventeen and Ready'. As Chris Carson was back on the ship and Ric Harris had left the Communicator. David Lee Stone took the breakfast show over from Ric as Chris hosted Stoner's hours in the afternoon.

On the 22nd Laser was in the newspapers again. This time in the locally Shropshire Star: 'The man behind the success of the pirate radio station Laser is to join Radio Luxembourg, which broadcasts programmes on '208' to Britain. He is 25-years old American deejay David Lee Stone. At Laser Mr. Stone has been responsible for broadcast style and music. Since he has been there it is claimed the station has taken listeners from BBC Radio, Radio Luxembourg and the Independent Local Radio. Announcing the appointment yesterday, Richard Swainson, Radio Luxembourg's head of Music, said: "David is one of that rare breed who combine great warmth and ability on air."

'Media Week' published the same day more than one page article about Laser in the George Pitcher column 'Up to a point': 'I read with more than usual interest an interview in Campaign, the advertising trade magazine, with one John Elliot. Elliot presents himself as spokesman for the pirate radio station Laser 558, and in addition to giving an interview to Campaign; uses notepaper headed Multimedia International. This is confusing, for I had understood that Laser's representative in the UK was in fact John Moss, of the company incidentally similarly named Music Media International. Moss describes Elliot as an 'overzealous job applicant', whom he has never met but who applied by phone for a job advertised by Laser, describing himself as a friend of the station. 'He wants to get into our knickers in some way', adds Moss. Should he succeed Moss may have cause to worry about his laundry bill.'

In a separate article about Laser Nick Higham wrote: 'Radio Laser itself has operated from at least two addresses in London. Using the cover name of 'Overseas Media Inc, it last year rented an office at the Kensington Business Centre at 9-11 Kensington High Street in London. The Business Centre provides accommodation and office services to clients. The Centre's Manager, Henning Grobein, confirmed that Overseas Media had rented an office there, but claimed it no longer did so. He would not say when Overseas Media had given up the premises. The address was known to the UK record companies, who used it to deliver records destined for airplay on Laser. As well as the Kensington Business Centre Laser also operates from an address in the Earls Court area of London, with phone number on which the station's manager, an American who calls himself 'John Charles', can be contacted. Charles has been in contact with a number of British record companies in the past seven months, asking them to keep Laser supplied with records.

Charles told Media Week: 'I don't have a visibility in the local press and my whereabouts are not bandied about, in order for me to touch base in various countries where we may not operate legally. If I came into England under my own identity the Government might not want me and might try to stop me.' Charles claimed to have managed a number of US radio stations and that he owned a station in Connecticut. Earlier this month he spent a fortnight on the ship, which is moored in the Thames Estuary just outside the 12-mile limit and close to the Ross Revenge from which rival pirate radio Caroline broadcasts. Before that he was touring in the US recruiting extra DJs, among them three women – to bring Laser's on air staff up to eight. Meanwhile New York based salesman John Moss was studiously vague last week about his reasons for being in London. He took over as president of Music Media International in December from Roy Lindau, the first president, who was apparently ousted because of the station's disappointing sales performance since October, when four months of avowedly commercial-free broadcasting came to an end. Moss, aged 30, is an energetic salesman with an impressive track record, who has worked for leading US radio rep house Blair Radi, CBS and the Radio Advertising Bureau.

Although Laser had carried advertisements for Ritz Magazine and has given name checks to other companies like Time Out and Trustee Savings Bank, Moss denies that any British companies advertise on the station. He denies that Laser is hypocritical in its claim to be legal when most observers believe it is supplied from the UK and that its crew is frequently enter the country without bothering going through the proper immigration channels. Moss said: 'The hypocrisy is in the rules that we are seen as being in contravention of. In the US broadcasters are the guardians of the airwaves. They have a responsibility to give the populace what they want. The marketplace dictates standards, the audience wants a service; and that's what radio is: a service. Laser has taken $250,000 in advertising since August and could be profitable with $100,000 a month revenue.'

On March 23rd both Liz West and Charlie Wolf paid attention to the fact that during that week their competitor Radio Caroline was celebrating the 21st birthday. Also, they asked the listeners for ideas how to celebrate their 1st birthday in May. Let's go to March 27th when at 8.44 we first heard a promo for 'I will return' by English Evenings. The station went off the air at approximately 13.30 that day during Chris Carson's programme and returned at about 14.40 with Charlie Wolf at the mike.

Laser and Caroline together 1985

Charlie continued up till 15.43 when Erin took over and closed her part of the programming at 17.00. Then a four hour show with Liz was heard, followed by the Seawolf till close down. Like on earlier offshore radio stations, nicknames were often heard on Laser 558. Chris Carson became known as 'C.C. Rider' and Liz West 'Dizzy Miss Lizzy.' The 29th brought us a new promo, 'The Soul of Cashmere' an album from Cashmere.

On March 29th also in an edition of a magazine called 'City Limits' an article was published that included an interview with David Lee Stone. Reporter Lyn Champion wrote: 'Actor, model, DJ and lead singer of an LA rock band, traded his former Californian lifestyle for an uncertain existence spinning records in the North Sea'. Lee Stone: "This is just an adventure. I didn't do it for the money, fame or fortune. In fact, I never really considered the idea of this thing turning into such a big-time deal. I knew I could always go back to California and get a job there. Now I would probably get one anywhere, having programmed Laser. I mean, it's so satisfying to be with a station that's so enormously successful that everywhere you go people are talking about it and listening to it. I could go back and be one in a million, but over here anyone who works for Laser is quickly becoming a name. You're listening to Planet Earth's most exciting new Radio Station! We play the best music and you know that too, don't you?"

That same day it was Charlie doing Chris Carson's programme as she – again – felt very sea-sick. On March 30th saw the start of the Arabian Sands Village Contest and Laser's neighbours on Caroline offered a similar package.

Not always smooth sailing

Chapter 13

STILL THERE, BUT ADRIFT

First, I thought it was an April Fool's Joke when I heard that David Lee Stone was on the air that day in the early morning hours. No Radio Luxembourg yet, as was written in the newspapers. He went on till 09.00 when Erin Kelly followed for four hours. At 13.00 it was Chris, 17.00 BST she was followed by Liz and the last show of the day was for Charlie Wolf. During the last week of March, he talked a lot about his forthcoming holiday, which would take him to Utah in the USA, where some of his roots were. Of course, it was April's Fools Day and the ladies on the ship talked a lot about several 'April Fools' which were done in the past all over the world. Also, they made a lot of parodies from which: 'Put your hand on the radio, feel the power and strength of Laser 558' was a very good one. When tuning in on April 2nd we learned that the Seawolf had left the MV Communicator for a well-earned holiday.

Charlie leaving meant that David Lee Stone was responsible for two shifts that day, the early morning and late evening one. The three Laserettes filled the rest of the day. But on the 3rd, it was decided that everyone did a five hour long show. Only a day later it changed again as Ric was back and was heard on his usual slot between 05.00 and 09.00. At 8.31 a new commercial was logged for a clothing company, Prism, which was in South-end on Sea.

David Lee Stone was heard between 13.00 and 17.00 and another change was Liz West in the late evening as Charlie left for shore. Highly promoted on air by Laser as well as Caroline was the dart competition to be held between both stations aboard the MV Ross Revenge, on April 7th. However, it was cancelled as the weather was too bad to go with a little dinghy from the Communicator to Caroline's home.

Nothing much changed in the following days but on the 9th a new promo for a record was heard, being 'Love me right now' by Rose Royce. On the 10th at 13.08 suddenly Tommy Rivers was heard telling about his skiing holiday in Austria and that he had also been in Portugal, finally ending up in England where he had discovered the game of snooker. Endless hours of games were broadcast those days on television in Great Britain. Apparently, he had met a certain Steve Davis, who became six times world champion in this game. Tommy said that he wanted to install a snooker table, mounted on gimbals, onboard the radio ship.

It was also mentioned in David Lee Stone's program the next day, at 13.08, that Tommy again talked about snooker and gave a plug for Coral Bookmakers, who were taking bets on the annual Embassy Championship, who at that time was taking place in Sheffield. At 15.00 hrs Tommy Rivers took over from David Lee Stone. For the next two hours he was on and gave another plug for Coral. This was the last time we heard David Lee Stone on Laser 558 as he left for Radio Luxembourg, where he was heard eight days later saying 'try to get my land legs back'.

There was no sign of abatement during the early morning of Friday the 12th and Ric Harris opened the programs at 05.00, but an hour later he had bad news as the mast and the antenna system were taking the strain and at 06.36 early listeners learned that the station went very abruptly off the air, without any warning by Ric himself. We later learned that the anchor had broken and the MV Communicator was adrift.

Within three hours the captain had not only started the engines, which many times gave a problem when the Communicator was for longer time anchored at one place, but also succeeded to get the ship to her original anchorage. He then secured the ship on the spare anchor. It was around 10.35 hrs that Erin reopened the program: "We finally found out what a wild world it is here out on the North Sea. We were off the air for just a little while because our aerial was whipping around just for a bit too much and we got knocked off the air for a little while. But thanks to our keen engineering crew we are back on the air and thanks to our Port Anchor we are back in position."

Later on, Erin returned with: "Have I got a story for you! With all this excitement, oddly enough 'David Lee Stone' slept through the whole thing! Wait till you hear what it did to Michael Dean though! Do you know the story of the last time we broke our mooring? Remember Michael Dean running to everyone's room and saying: "Wake up; we're all going to die"?

Well, we got him back today. I wasn't there for that one, but I was here for this: Hmm Hmm! We woke Michael up by singing 'Amazing Grace' and telling him: "Michael, wake up, we're all going to die". But we didn't and we knew we wouldn't, because we've got an Able Bodied Seaman staff right here on board. Ok, I confess; we didn't know that we weren't definitely going to die. You know, you never know about that. It was just us against the sea, the hands of the Sailors against the Sea. Pretty dramatic, huh? I guess it was. It was a lot of fun too, but there's nothing you can do except to wait and see. So, with that in mind here's the Jam with 'Funeral Pyre' on Laser!"

Erin Kelly

Later on, Erin told her listeners that it had all been 'a put on': "What excitement! Getting the pictures of all the sailors and the Laserettes and the DJs. And we got it all on film, so now we know for sure it wasn't fantasy; that is of course if the film doesn't turn up. No really, it really did happen, I promise you!"

It was fortunate that the station did get back on the air that day for the five winners for the Arabian Sands Holiday, which would be announced that afternoon. When the names were finally mentioned, those listeners had only 30 minutes to claim their prices by a collect call to the New York office of Music Media International. The next day nothing happened. On the 13th we heard the first mentioning of 'the Laser Glass Wall'. Listeners were asked to send their personal photo to be pinned at this wall on board the MV Communicator. With the recent tender also some 'thank you for playing our record' spots had arrived, including one from the Thompson Twins and Rose Royce. April 15th brought a very sunny day as well as Erin back on the deck making photographs of deejays and crew. She later told us that the deck was bathed in sun and that they had decided it was the official start of Eurotan '85.

Let's go back to the press to a well-known financial magazine, called 'Forbes', which was released in the third week of April 1985: 'It's an old story. Government thinks it knows best and kills competition, until entrepreneurs figure how to give people what they want while making dollars at it. This time the story is being played in the North Sea on an old survey ship anchored 14 miles from Britain. There, Charlie Wolf, a disc jockey from Utah, and seven American cronies risk the gales to run Laser 558, a new radio station backed by US investors. It plays hit music, advertises US goods and shakes up broadcasters across Europe. "We're having a marvellous time here on the high seas, and we're doing a fever pitch", says Charlie.

The BBC supported by taxes on TV sets, insists it's not worried about the challenge, but London's top commercial station stole a Laser DJ and brought in live music to win back listeners. "They didn't know, what competition was," says Charlie Wolf, the DJ from Provo.

April 17th brought us two new promos for records, the first for Barbara Pennington's new single 'Fan the flame', followed by 'The ABC of kissing' by Richard Jon Smith. EMI and Callard and Bowser were just two of the companies that had won 'Cleo Awards', the equivalent of and 'Oscar' for commercials originally broadcast in the States. A re-run was started of the examples on these on April the 18th on Laser, each of which concluded with a Laser deejay saying: 'Congratulations to... for the effective use of Radio Advertising' and then giving MMI's telephone number with the instructions to ask for

'Brad'. These examples, of which there were a dozen of on board the Communicator, were first heard in 1984 on Laser.

On the 19th, at 17.46 we heard the first commercial for Worldwide Student Travel. On the 19th around 19.10, during the Liz West programme, we heard for the first time from the 'spiritual adviser', 'Beulah the Towel-Head', which was in reality Tommy Rivers. Beulah began his regular appearances at 17.15 to answer 'stupid cosmic questions' on Monday the 22nd. As no questions had at that time been received from listeners, the privilege fall to the cook, Michal Dean, to ask the first question: "where does the spam come from?" Beulah assured him that Spam comes from a Spam animal, which is a cross between a pig and an aardvark and was invented in a warehouse in Buffalo New York! This type of answers became the order of the day on Monday, Tuesday, Thursday and Friday each week. It didn't appear in the 'Laser Chart Action', which was featured on the Wednesdays at Laser 558. The same day a new record promo was heard for 'Rage to love' by Kim Wilde. Finally, to mention about the 22nd was that the North Sea was in the worsening storm conditions. Chris Carson only managed to complete the first two hours of her planned four-hour programme and it was Michael Dean, who came to rescue her.

All the above loggings bring us to Tuesday the 23rd of April. We heard Ric Harris at normal time – between 05.00 and 09.00, followed by Erin Kelly up till 13.00. She was followed by Tommy Rivers and he continued his programme, despite the increasing ferocity of a North- Easterly storm until 16.50 hrs, when the forward mast again buckled, putting Laser once again off the air. Probably Laser 558 became with this the number one station in the History of Offshore Radio in getting lost their transmitter mast during several storms. It was also the last logging for the month of April as in the then forthcoming weeks no signal was heard on '558' and people on the ship were working hard to erect a brand new foremast on the MV Communicator.

Chapter 14

ALMOST A YEAR 'ON AIR'

May 1985 saw the celebrations for Laser 558 being on the air for one year. Those who followed the station know that they had many breakdowns, so officially the station was less than a year on 558. Let's see what was happening in the month of May 1985.

May 1st saw an article in the London Standard mentioning that 'Pirate radio ship Laser 558 has hired a new disc jockey – a distant cousin of the Prince of Wales, Alan Stewart-Wortley Bishop, 25, who began spinning the discs on the station this week said: "We're blood relatives. You'll find my name in Burke's Peerage.' At the time the Department of Trade and Industry (DTI) raids on inland pirate stations are on the increase. Laser lies 20 miles off the Kent coast outside territorial waters and beyond the reach of British law. And under the 1967 Marine Offences Act the Government takes a dim view of anyone supplying, assisting, working for, and listening to an unlicensed station. Alan's arrival onboard is bound to cause some embarrassment. "Diana and I share the same great, great, great grandfather, a pork packer from Ohio, called John Wood. The family seat is in Wortley, near Sheffield, and my uncle is her earl quite well. They write to each other and my parents stayed with him when they visited England last year."

Alan has just arrived first class by Virgin Airline from New York. He will spend the next two months aboard the MV Communicator, a 180 foot former Lowestoft fishing trawler, home of Laser 558. He has a degree in business studies and spent two years working for radio stations in Detroit and Worchester, Massachusetts, before landing his new job last week. Before setting sail the station's new DJ said: "I discovered my bloodline when Charles and Diana were married. An aunt of mine in Seattle got a call from two American authors who have written a book called 'American Ancestors and cousins of the Princess of Wales'. My name is my mother's former maiden name. She has told me that we are also descendants of Mary Stuart, Queen of Scots. On the air, though, I'll be using a false name like all the other DJ's. I'm calling myself Craig Novack." '

We knew already less sensational of the arrival from Craig Novack as a letter was sent out by MMI coming in late April in which was mentioned: 'Laser Radio welcomes new DJ Craig Novack, the Amazing Colossal DJ. Craig is 25 years old at 6 feet 5 inches, the biggest guy you will hear on the radio. Craig grew up in Bath, Maine, graduated from Syracuse University and started his radio career in Syracuse, New York at WFBL AM, the first hot hits radio station in the U.S. His other radio postings include the seven to midnight show on WHYT Detroit, owned by Capital Cities, and most recently he was an advertising representative WFTQ-AM in Worchester. '

On May the 7th, a Tuesday, at 13.28 the transmitter was switched on and off several times until 13.55 when a tuning tone was put out. This continued until 14.30 when non-stop music commenced. At 15.00 programming restarted. Officially it was Tommy Rivers' programme, but for the first hour of their comeback he was aided and abetted by Liz West, Chris Carson and new DJ Craig Novack. Tommy: "Welcome to Laser 558, we've been having a lot of fun out here for the last two weeks. We've learned how to work on the deck; we learned how to rebuild the mast." Liz: "And we've learned how to work on the deck – and then we learned how to on the deck and then: ...Oh, we got a new deejay. I'm sure you've read about him in the papers..."

Tommy: "He's near royalty, right Craig?" Craig: "Near royalty, that's right. Chris Carson is royalty and I'm sitting right next to her." Chris: "Oh boy, what can I say?" Craig: "I think it was great, Liz, how you put that new mast up for us. It was hard work over two weeks but I think that now that it is up and the fact that you put it up, it's never coming down again." Liz: "That's right! We've got the new, industrial-strength, new and improved mast; this will never come down." Craig: "And the thing is, it's held up by garter-straps, right?" Chris: "And the thing is, Liz sacrificed three of her fingernails for this venture and I would just like to take this time to, you know, have a second of memory for those fingernails that you so lovingly gave for the cause." Liz: "That's right! And there's dirt under the rest, the remaining seven fingernails – which has never happened in my entire lifetime!" Craig: "Are we supposed to have a moment of silence now for your fingernails?" Liz: "I think we've had more than enough silence!" Tommy: "Yeah, I think you're right, let's go back to some tunes."

At 17.30 Tommy's programme ended on that day, then Liz West took the microphone to present for the next 2, 5 hours. Between 20.00 and 22.30 Craig Novack presented his first show, followed by Chris Carson till closedown time at 01.00. Throughout the day the card numbers of the Communicator Club Members were being read out. Their owners were to receive the new Prince Album and two bonus albums if they wrote to the station's New York address, quoting the time their name and number were read out on the station.

For the first four or five days after the resumption of broadcasting a forthcoming party for the station's first birthday that was to take place at the London Hippodrome was heavily promoted, where the live sound of Laser 558 would be piped to the assembled multitude. Then the announcement suddenly stopped without an explanation. With only a week to go before the event The Party was taken over by Club Eighteen -Thirty. We had to wait until Friday the 31st for an explanation to the birthday party mystery which was provided by the London Standard. 'No Pirate beams for Laser. Pirate radio station Laser 558 was scuppered when it tried to put on a first birthday party at the Hippodrome last week. The day after the proposed party was advertised on the air a police officer paid a visit to the publicity conscious club owner Peter Stringfellow, warning him not to stage the event.

The party had been arranged by the Laser spokeswomen Jane Morris during a recent visit to London from her New York base. "The police came over very tough and very strong. We were left in no doubt that this party would have to be cancelled and that action would be taken if it wasn't", says Stringfellow. "I was happy to accept the party booking at first because I didn't think there was anything wrong. It wasn't one of those things I wanted to take a political stance over." The police action was prompted by the Department of Trade and Industry who are responsible for monitoring pirate stations. When they heard on the radio about the party, they contacted the director of Public Prosecutions to warn them it could be in breach of the law. "It was up to the DPP what action would follow our information", says a DTI spokeswoman.'

Let's go back to the programme logs and we heard on May the 8th Craig Novack doing the breakfast show up till 10.00 and during the programme he introduced a new item that would become a regular one. 'How to talk American', in which he explained the meaning of various slang expressions in those days in use in the U.S. After Craig, Tommy Rivers showed up for the presentation of the hours up till 15.00. During his show we heard a record promo for 'True life confessions' by a group called 'The Korgis'. From 15.00 up till 20.00 it was time to listen to Liz West again and she presented the very first Laser chart show, Euro Hit Survey. The final five hours, for that day, were presented by Chris Carson. The following day another new plug was heard for 'People Magazine' as well as for 'Seven is really hot'.

The London Standard wasn't afraid for the MOA as they had another article on Laser 558 on May the 10th, which was again an interesting read: "The increasing links between the North Sea pirate radio station Laser 558 and music tycoon Richard Branson will be of great interest to the Department of Trade and Industry. Branson's Virgin Atlantic Airlines is now supplying Laser disc jockeys and crew with free first-class transatlantic air tickets. In return the airline receives numerous commercials beamed to the station's estimated 5.000.000 strong audience around Britain and Europe. Since no money changes hands and the work is handled through Virgin's Atlantic Office in New York, the deal does not contravene the 1967 Marine Offences Act, which forbids commercial dealings by British companies with pirate radio outfits."

"Millionaire Branson, who admits that he has looked into ways of taking over Laser, is coy about the exact Laser-Virgin connection. "If my airline looks after Laser DJ's, and as long as it's not breaking any law it sounds like an admirable arrangement. I don't know every single marketing or promotional activity of the airline, but I do know that Laser has been kind to the airline on the airwaves and I could possibly put two and two together." Virgin is not the only British Company co-operating with Laser. Time Out Magazine is also in on the game with the station using the Magazines gig-listening section in return for plugging Time Out on the air. Says a Time Out spokesman: "We are totally sympathetic with the liberalisation of the airwaves and we are 100 percent behind Laser. Its 5.000.000 listeners prove it is exactly what people have wanted for ages."

On May the 10th also plug was heard for the American Gay Group 'Village People', which would be appearing at Rain's Disco, which was then a well visited venue in Southend-on-Sea. During the evening Chris Carson ended her program earlier and this had a reason as during the evening a tender had brought Charlie Wolf back to the MV Communicator. He probably missed making radio as he did not close down Laser 558 at 01.00, that night, but went on up till 2.37! Of course, with Charlie back in the schedule and no one leaving, there were four hour long programs again with 05.00 till 09.00 Craig Novack, 09.00-13.00 Chris Carson in the seat, followed by Tommy Rivers. At 17.00 Liz West who was followed for the rest of the night, from 21.00 on, by Charlie Wolf. Also, this time Charlie couldn't stop in time as his last words were heard that night at 01.15.

On Tuesday the 14th, for the first time after coming back on the air again, a break in transmissions was heard from 20.53 up till 21.14. No reason was given. An advert for Sandy Student Travel Service was for the first time logged. That same evening we heard for the first time a particularly amusing 'spoof' advert. It was enacted by astronauts talking to mission control, and the answer to all their problems was to drink 'Farrah' beer. The first half of the month of May 1985 was notable for the invasion on the Communicator by large numbers of pigeons – some of them even getting into cabins and studios.

On the 15th a new record promo was heard, this time the song 'Second Nature' by Dan Hartman was recommended. That day the Euro Hit Survey show with Liz West already carried another name as it was changed into: 'Laser Chart Action.' During her programme there was a short breakdown due to problems with 'Alice the generator', as Liz told at 18.33. Another record promo was heard the next day: La Bouche and the song 'Romantic Love'. On May 17th we heard the first of a new series of advertisements marking the birthday of Virgin Atlantic Airlines. Around that time also the 'Laser Spot Song' was introduced in the programmes. This was a kind of station's hit pick appearing several times a day. The deejays also announced that the 'Laser Spot Song' were paid advertisements.

On May the 19th programmes went normal till 17.00 and Tommy Rivers, who normally ended his programme at that time, extended it till 18.00. Liz followed till 20.05. Not a normal time but we learned not much later that she suddenly left the radio ship with a tender. So, Tommy Rivers was back in the chair until 21.00 when Charlie took over. A new commercial was heard that day for 'Human to Human' from the formation 'Adja'. The tender brought Ric Harris back to the ship. He was away for 26 days and the next morning he was back on his normal shift, doing the breakfast show. There was another change in programming as May 20th saw Craig Novack taking over the hours which Liz left behind, 17.00 – 21.00. This however happened without the assistance of Beulah the Towelhead, which we became used to.

We had another good laugh on the 21st when Charlie Wolf played at 23.12 for the first time an advert for 'Ross Revenge Luxury Estates', and he announced that he was staying over there! The next day the programming was a bit chaotic. Tommy was heard at 10.00 in the morning instead of Chris Carson and went on till 11.00 when Erin Kelly reappeared after a 28 days break, in which she had some holiday, including a visit to Paris. She was relieved at 13.40 by Craig because a film crew was on the MV Communicator and presumably her presence was required for that. Craig programmed until 17.00 and then Chris took over for the Laser Chart Action. For the first two hours Craig stayed in the studio to assist Chris Carson with her very first top 40 show. That day we also heard the first promo for the song: 'Sorry, wrong number', by Evelyn Thomas.

On the 23rd a bit more regular programming came in again with 05.00 till 08.43 Ric, then Erin till 12.00. The next three hours were presented by Tommy 'What a guy' Rivers. 15.00 up till 18.30 we heard Craig, which was followed up till 21.07 by Chris Carson. The remaining hours for that day were presented by Charlie Wolf. That day also a new record promo was heard: 'New Beginning', by Force Eight. How many of those record promo's really became a hit?

May 24th came and as we told before it was the day to celebrate that Laser 558 was 'One'. Unfortunately, the rough weather afflicting the Knock Deep at the time reduced the numbers of expected guests to the shipboard party but that wasn't allowed to spoil the atmosphere on the air. All programmes were outstanding pieces of entertainment. The entire Laser jingle package was played several times throughout the day, and we were also treated to excerpts from the tape of Laser 558's first ever programme one year earlier – a programme that almost everyone on land missed at the time, as it had begun at five o'clock in the morning with no prior announcement. At noon listeners in the London area were promised a special treat. A banner-towing aircraft was to be aloft for about an hour, its streamer proclaiming 'Happy Birthday Laser 558'. Charlie became almost crazy at 23.00 when he shot BBC Radio One off the air. Playing a Radio One jingle he mixed it halfway with the sound of a riffle.

On Saturday May 25th The Times came with an article entitled 'How pirates could rescue radio'. It was written by John Catlett, general manager of Laser 558: 'Laser Radio is called 'a pirate'. This is picturesque, picaresque description; but wrong. Laser Radio may be buccaneering, operating as it does from a ship in international waters, but it breaks no laws. In Britain is it accused of 'stealing' its frequency – 558 metres medium wave – because that is one of dozens of frequencies allocated to, but not used by the BBC. Laser selected the frequency with care to avoid interference with existing stations and communications essential to marine safety, following the tradition of Radio Luxembourg and Vatican Radio, both of which broadcast long before they achieved the sanction of any international body. As it celebrates its first birthday, the station has gained five million listeners a week in Britain. Commercial radio in Britain is in a mess. With a few notable exceptions it fails to deliver what advertisers and listeners want. It tries to be all things to all people: local and national, music and information orientated, aimed at young and old.'

'In trying to serve so many masters it serves no one well. Different people want different things from radio. The costs of producing radio programmes are so low and so many frequencies are available that there is no good reason to deprive the public of as many different radio services and creative minds can devise. Why is that New York, a city smaller than London, can support more than 70 radio stations when in London only 7 can officially be heard? This is not a matter of physics but of politics and vested interests. Laser Radio is programmed in belief that a certain section of the European population want to hear hit music uninterrupted by talk. Many people have no desire to listen to a station such as Laser and their tastes should be met elsewhere. But many millions do want such a station. Who after all owns the frequencies – the government's broadcasting organisations or the people themselves?'

'The most vocal critic of Laser in Britain is to be found in the independent, commercial radio industry. Are they really, as they claim, trying to protect the excellence of British commercial radio or are they simply trying to protect their monopoly? Laser is attacked for not paying copyright fees. This is hardly the fault of the station; we would be delighted to pay. Record companies and artists are only too happy to have their music on the air. It is their collection agencies which refuse payment because they lack jurisdiction on the high seas. The station is devoted to musical entertainment. It has not and will not broadcast political or religious propaganda. We observe our own strict rules on advertising and good taste and operate with the highest technical standards, possible for a marine station. Commercial radio attracts little more than two percent of all advertising expenditure in Britain. In America, where the figure is nearer eight percent, the radio industry is vibrant and strong. Commercial radio there succeeds by providing what people want. Rather than fighting Laser's existence, British radio stations should welcome the competition and work with us to improve standards on commercial radio. Then perhaps Britain's radio as well as its television will be the envy of the world.'

Chris Edwards of OEM asked John Catlett about his location and he disclosed that he spent the majority of his time in England. "Laser's owning company is Panamanian but was run from England. It had an affiliation with an American sales company, MMI."

When asked who was involved in the organisation in England: "I was involved, but there were some people who wished to remain anonymous. I hired the disc jockeys and kept track of who was due to be paid anything and what advertising there was to go on the air. We had substantial sales help, most of our sales activity occurred here and it was in the summer of 1985 that I closed down the offices in New York and moved them to a very much smaller space along the street at 515 Madison Avenue because we were spending at the time more money on the New York sales office than we were on the ship and the entire crew and it made no kind of sense to have that kind of expenditure.'

On the 25th we heard the promo for 'TV Glare' by Absolute. Tommy Rivers and Liz West left the ship for a holiday that day so, the programming for the 26th was 05.00 till 09.00 Ric Harris, 09.00 – 13.00 Erin Kelly, followed by Craig Novack. At 17.00 we heard Chris Carson and the last segment for the day started at 21.00 with Charlie Wolf. On May 28th we heard for the first time the commercial for the International edition of 'USA Today'. The next day there was a breakdown in transmissions and Erin explained: "We had a little trouble with the generator so we thought we'd switch off for a while just so we didn't explode." The Laser Chart Action, which was programmed that day in the afternoon, again was presented by Chris and Craig.

Chapter 15

NEGATIVE NEWSPAPER SUPPORT

June 1985 started with the message from the MMI Office that official investigation was made at the office from Time Magazine to find out if there were any links to the Laser organisation. As far as they knew at the time, nothing was found by the DTI people. On Monday June 3rd we heard another record promo, this time for 'The cat is out', performed by Judie Tzuke. So, money was still coming in from record companies.

The same day again a celebration took place as it was Craig Novak's birthday. The next morning several plugs were read out for a book, written by Derby Day and published by Coral Bookmakers. But more happened as a severe storm prevailed throughout the day and between 19.08 and 19.50 the transmitter was switched off 'To allow things to dry out". Also, a record promo for 'Buttercup', a song by Carl Anderson was heard. Next to records and books other plugs appeared, like on June the 6th when we heard for the first time at 17.50 a plug for a movie called 'Witness the Daily Star', with Harrison Ford in the main male role. It was of course another production from United Artists movie department. It was not until the 10th that another new record promo was heard and it was 'summer the first time' by Kenny Copeland. Two days later we logged for the first time a commercial for a London based holiday agency: 'North American Travel'.

On the 12th, the Laser Chart Action show was co-presented by Chris Carson and Erin Kelly and this would also happen the next Wednesday. On June the 13th we just listened for a short period to Laser 558 and heard another new commercial for 'North America Travel' travelling with discount prices. On April 14th another record promo appeared regularly for April and 'Boys come and go'. June 16th brought a late evening travel with the dinghy by some of the Laser crew to the Ross Revenge to have a drink or two as the Radio Monique crew celebrated the fact, they were 6 months on the air and wanted this to share with their competitors.

On the evening of June 17th, a break in transmission was noted between 20.18 and 20.35 during Chris Carson's show. From the 19th a change to the station's address was being announced. It became Laser Radio, P.O. Box 1828, Grand Central Station, New York City,. USA. On Sunday June 23rd Ric presented his last ever breakfast show for Laser 558. That evening Charlie Wolf was conspicuous by his absence from the 21.00 – 01.00 slot. Instead, we heard non-stop music with the following recorded announcement inserted twice in every hour: "I'm Ric Harris speaking on behalf of the management of Laser 558. We apologise for any irregularities you may notice in this evening's Charlie Wolf Fever-Pitch radio programme. As you may already know, contract negotiations between Eurad SA and Mr. Wolf are reaching a critical stage. A work action has been threatened, and if one does occur be assured that the loyal staff and management of Laser shall make every effort to maintain normal services. Thank you."

As Ric left the station without a replacement, programming went back to 5 hours slots. From the 24th we had Craig at breakfast, followed at 10.00 by Erin Kelly. Then at 15.00 Chris Carson followed and at 20.00 we heard Charlie till closedown time. He made no references at all to the curious announcements the previous evening.

Craig Novack

On June 26th another record promo appeared in the programs for 'The Warrior', a song by The New York Connection. Readers of the London Evening Standard could read an article the same evening with the header 'Is Laser's beam fading away?' 'Laser 558 is facing a financial crisis that threatens to take it permanently off the air within weeks. The North Sea's pirate radio station was forced this week to leave its smart offices in Manhattan's Madison Avenue for a smaller base. And is has had difficulties meeting bills, including those of the public relations consultant Jane Morris. Jane is coy to say how much Laser owes her but admits that Laser is 'not the world's best payer and I'm not in the business of providing my services without remuneration.' Now, in a week that has seen the departure of yet another Laser disc jockey – Ric Harris has defected to Ireland's successful pirate station, Radio Nova – other DJs aboard the MV Communicator are believed to be seeking new jobs. Laser's latest crisis follows the collapse of advertising from American multi-national companies.

With 3, 5 million Pounds already spent on the operation, the station's main backer reclusive Irish Businessman Philip Smyth, is reluctant to part with more cash. Morale on the ship is said to be at an all-time low and has not been helped by Laser's new policy of 'spotlighting', where companies pay for their records to be played, which has upset several DJ's.'

On June 27th alterations in program times were again taking place. Craig ended his breakfast show an hour earlier, when Chris was heard up till 14.00. Then Erin followed till 19.00. The first half of hour of her show contained complete album sides due, so she explained, to the fact that work was to be done on the transmitter. The final six hours of the day were presented by Charlie.

The following day saw the return of Liz West and Tommy Rivers. So next to Craig at breakfast we heard from 10.00 till 15.00 Erin. From 15.00 – 17.00 Tommy Rivers was assisted by Liz West. They had both been on holiday together in Morocco, after which Liz spent a week in a London's hospital recovering from dysentery! She commented that this was a most unpleasant disease: "Opens the sluices at both ends".

After 17.00 the next 54 minutes brought us Liz West solo, and then up till 21.00 Tommy Rivers joined her again. Liz's job was not ready as she went on till close down time at 01.00. That taught us too that Charlie had left the Communicator. Also, Michael Dean left the ship and was replaced by Stuart Vincent, who was involved earlier and also worked some spells as a technician on board the MV Ross Revenge of Radio Caroline.

On the 29th of June we were very surprised to hear a promo for 'Telstar power boat' for the very first time, tuned by Laser and powered by Chevrolet engines. It was to take part in a race from London docks to Ramsgate. At 08.42 the Laser drag-racing team was first mentioned, coupled with a plug for the Carburettor Centre. The same day we also heard for the first time a commercial for a Dutch Album release, available from a postal address in the Hague, containing 25 top tracks costing 10 Pounds, including packing and postage.

On June the 30th, a Sunday, Liz West's program was cut short at 22.00 hrs when we heard the birth of a new sponsored syndicated programme from the USA presented by Scott Shannon. 'Rocking America Top 30' was a three hour programme and became from that date a regular Sunday show on Laser 558. It was a widely distributed syndicated show from Hollywood, produced by the Westwood One Radio Network.

During the first day of the month of July 1985 two new commercials were heard. The first one was aired just before eight o'clock in the morning. It was for 'Blast', computer software that in those days was a translator from Basic into machine code. The second one was aired for the first time at 10.49 which promoted the sea ferry between Flushing and Southend on Sea v.v., run by the Olau Line. On the promoted spot there was also a mentioning of the Laser Road Show aboard the ferry.

July 2nd brought programming back to 4 hours slots, starting which Craig, followed at 09.00 by Erin Kelly. At 13.00 we heard Tommy Rivers and then at 17.00 it was Liz West, presenting Beulah the Towelhead – having returned to the Communicator, as a regular spot at 17.15 answering stupid questions with even more stupid answers. At 21.00 hrs to close down, we heard a brand new Laserette, Jonell, who had come from Minnesota. She was a radio announcer at KTOE, originally a country station. She made contact with Laser through Tommy Rivers with whom she had worked in the States. After working for a year in Europe, Tommy decided to recruit Jonell for a short period. They needed some fill-in help for the summer, basically for only a two months period.

On July 3rd, a Wednesday, the Laser Chart Action was presented between 17.00 and 19.00 hrs by Liz West alone, which she also did for the remaining weeks in July. A day later a new commercial was heard for a double album called 'Artist Two'. We read another article in the press about Laser, this time in 'Broadcast': 'Laser 558 has been suffering from cash flow problems and its DJs have had to wait four to six weeks for their pay. The difficulties were caused by the shut-down in May to repair the antenna, badly battered by last winter's storm. "All funds were diverted to making the repairs", said John Moss, the President of MMI in New York. "I've personally gone several weeks without being paid." He said that the jocks and crew have now been paid. "Collectibles are coming in and there are enough orders on the book for us to continue", he added. His company has moved into a smaller office suite. This is because its earlier offices were not fully used rather than being due to financial stringency. The new office is still on Madison Avenue."

On Saturday July the 6th Jonell only presented a one hour show, from 21.00 to 22.00. That day saw the start a new series of recorded programs. It was 'Off the Record', a syndicated show presented by Mary Turner, a leading specialist in interviewing pop-stars and groups. In her first program, she interviewed Annie Lennox and Dave Stewart of the Eurythmics.

They had a problem on the Communicator as those syndicated show had several long intervals, to be filled with station's own promotions, jingles and commercials. By at the end of the program with Mary Turner there was a 10 minute gap, as Laser had so few commercials to insert between the several segments of the three hours show. It was filled by a block of 10 minutes of non-stop music until 22.00 hrs when the last show for the day started.

Yet another syndicated show, which was heard for the first time and which was, at that stage, very popular in the US. 'Dr Demento Show' was a program comprising weird and comedy songs. It was only heard once that month and we had a gap of five weeks before we could all get demented again. Like the Scott Shannon programme, both syndicated shows came in from syndicator 'Westwood One Radio Networks' in Hollywood.

Did Laser subscribe to the syndicated programs? Tommy Rivers: "John Moss was an old pal of Scott Shannon. I'm not sure where from, but John had worked American network radio sales out of New York for years and Scott Shannon was a big-shot disc-jockey not only in New York, but in Miami etc. He told Shannon the whole thing what this pirate operation was all about and Scott thought it was incredibly cool. About that time, he was doing 'Rocking America Top 30 Countdown, which was distributed by Westwood One. Each week, we'd get sent Westwood One products, including Dr Demento and the others. We weren't charged for it and we started putting this stuff out at weird hours during the week but we got it because John Moss knew Scott Shannon."

"Interestingly enough, a couple of years later Scott Shannon left New York and went to Los Angeles and was programme controller of a station there called PIRATE FM and he based the concept on what Moss had told him and what tapes he had heard about Laser and he tried to make a legitimate land-based station sound like a pirate. Obviously, it didn't work that well but that's where the seed for that whole idea came from and there were like mini 'pirates' all around America for a few years. You don't see that now but it was around in the late eighties everyone wanted to be a pirate but it was just a facade. You can't really be a pirate if you're a legitimate land- based radio station."

The next day we heard from one of our contacts that during the past week two ships, which were thought to be tenders for the radio ships, were stopped and searched by the British authorities. On one of the tenders was a lot of communication equipment including a new telex and so this one never arrived on board of one of the two radio ships. 'On a crowded street' was the title for another record promo, which was first heard on the 8th of July. It was a song by Barbara Pennington.

Buster Pearson informed me that on the same day an article was published in the London Standard, which read: 'The troubles at the North Sea pirate radio station Laser 558 are beginning to abate, according to their leading disc jockey Charlie Wolf. Mutinous mutterings had been heard on the ship with hold-ups of the salary cheques and continual problems with the transmitters. At one stage, reception was so weak that the deejays named the station Radio Margate. "There has been a crisis, but it's sorting itself out", says

Boston born Wolf, 26. 'Obviously the company is not making the millions they originally meant to, which is why they can't afford their prestigious Madison Avenue offices. However, advertising seems to be picking up."

From the 9th of July another address was mentioned for listener mail: Music Media International, 515 Madison Avenue, New York, N.Y. 10012 USA. Promos were also heard for the new Nils Lofgren album and a personal namecheck for Tommy Rivers, spoken by Dave Edmunds. On July 10th, Liz West told listeners about a popularity poll, published in the Melody Maker. Best DJ award went to John Peel, followed by Janice Long, Steve Wright and Ann Nightingale and in fifth place was the complete Laser DJ team.

On July 11th, we learned that Laser had now got an office at 7 Kensington High Street in west London, which was manned by John Cole and Robbie Day and known by the name of 'Overseas Media Incorporated'.

Some things to mention regarding July the 13th, which was a Saturday: Jonell started her evening show normally at 21.00 and the first hour was devoted to 'Rock Across America', sponsored by Marlboro cigarettes. Then between 22.00 and 23.00 another edition of the Mary Turner program, this time with an interview with the Kinks. Jonell returned at 23.00 to present the two final hours for that day.

'The three John's advert', a new spot for Virgin Atlantic Airways, was heard for the first time on July 16th. In the spot a mentioning of John, John and Johan, who were all heading for the airport of Maastricht, where the Virgin planes also had a line. The spot included the phone number of the Maastricht office.

Three days later, on the 19th, another new advertisement was heard. It was for a W.H. Smith publication called 'Music Master'. On Saturday the 20th, Mary Turner's interview was with the members of U2, an Irish band. They later became famous from 1987 when their album Joshua Tree became a massive global hit.

Advertisers from all kinds of places came in, mostly with very short runs. In this category were 'La Matre Fireworks' of Purley Way in Croydon Surrey. Another new one was for 'King's Country Club' in Eastbourne. They were heard for the first time on July 22nd. Next day saw another new record plugged for the first time in a so called 'paid promo'. It was Jeff Dean and the Tropical Fish and their song: 'Holiday Inn'.

On July 23rd, Craig Novak presented his breakfast show between 05.00 and 09.00 and then left the ship. This meant a reshuffle in programming and from the next day the schedule brought us Jonell on breakfast, followed at 09.00 by Erin Kelly, 13.00 Tommy Rivers, 17.00 Liz West and at 21.00 Charlie Wolf, who had returned on the MV Communicator. We also noted that was the day that a new commercial for 'La Fature', lightning equipment, was heard.

On July 25th for the first time an advertisement for the International Business Centre in London including a so called 'Personal Hi Fi Offer', for a Sanyo NGR 60. Not much later the same company had the first promo for an LP called 'Soul Giants'. Late in the evening, at 22.00, there was another edition of the Mary Turner program, interviewing another, then new one, in the pop-scene, Huey Lewis. July 26th, which was a Friday, brought us for the first time between 21.00 and 22.00 hrs. 'Salute to Motown.' The last thing that month of July was a late start in programming on the 30th. It was not before 05.17 that Jonell began her show as she had overslept.

Charlie Wolf

Chapter 16

BEEB AID - NOT LIVE AID

August 1985 began with the launch of 'a new charity' by Charlie Wolf using the name 'Beeb Aid'. He was very concerned to hear about the economy cuts the BBC had to make in their broadcasting budget. He felt that if 'Live Aid' could save thousands from the devastating drought in Ethiopia, then 'Beeb Aid' was just what was needed to prevent such horrors as Radio Four becoming Radio Two if everything at the BBC was halved. That would mean Radio One becoming Radio a Half or Radio 0.5. Radio Three would be absorbed by the BBC World Service or might even disappear completely! It was Charlie's intention to make a record to sell for the cause, and he was delighted to be able to announce that their friends on the 'Ross Revenge' had promised not only to join in on this effort but also to donate several thousand gallons of their home brew 'GBH Bitter' to the project.

Things ran normally on Laser 558 until the evening when Liz West finished her program at 20.28. They thought it was half past because their studio clock was two minutes fast, and had been for the past few days. It was Charlie Wolf who took over, explaining that they would be closing down at eleven o'clock in the evening to enable the engineers to make improvements to the transmitter. He also mentioned that they would not be on the air on the regular 05.00 o'clock but that at least 07.00 the next morning.

When the station closed down there was a new sign-off song introduced, which was 'When you wish upon a star', a song from 1940 sung by Cliff Edwards from the movie 'Pinocchio'. Directly after that recorded close-down announcement followed in which we were informed that the station would re-open the next morning at five; followed by some 'quacking' sound effects. Some minutes of dead silence followed when the microphone was opened and someone, calling himself 'the Janitor' was requesting the listener to 'scram' so that he could clean up the studios and let the engineers get on with their work. The Janitor was one of the many 'voices' used by the SeaWolf during his time on Laser 558. The transmitter went off the air that evening at 23.10 hrs.

The next day, which was a Friday, started at 05.37 when Jonell opened the station. She apologised for the late start and blamed it on the previous nights 'celebrations' over at the 'Ross', where a great deal of the famous 'GBH' brew had been consumed. From 10.00 Erin Kelly was on for three hours, followed by Tommy Rivers. Then from 16.00 till 18.30 Liz West was in the seat and from 18.30 up till 23.00 it was Charlie Wolf on air. Again, it was announced that they were closing early for engineering work on the transmitters; the Janitor once more closed down the station around the top of the hour and the transmitter was switched off at 23.08 that evening.

From this day on, the new address for letters was mentioned more frequently. Listeners were asked to write to 'PO Box 1828 Grand Central Station New York'. A new cook was presented the same day, Fiona Jefferies, who earlier had worked on the Ross Revenge, where she also did some radio shows.

August 3rd the transmitter was on at 06.43 and Jonell was heard from 07.00 till 10.00, followed for three hours each by Erin Kelly and Tommy Rivers. Liz was on between 16.00 and 19.30 and she sounded particularly depressed during her program. On one occasion, when she was given out the station's new address she added: "If you were thinking of sending us some money or food you can do so and add a dedication at the same time." Then later, when it was time for her to announce competition prizes, she slipped in: "We're giving away our general manager's apartment.

After Liz up till 21.58 (the clock was still running two minutes ahead on the Communicator) Charlie was heard and as it was a Saturday he was followed by Mary Turner, who that time had an interview with John Fogerty. This program went on till 22.50 hrs when the sign-off tape was played and the transmitter was switched off at 22.57hrs.

The next day it was totally silence on 558 as the last radio tube on the Communicator had blown and a new one had to be brought to the ship. On August the 5th listeners waited all day until a carrier appeared at 17.53 in the late afternoon. Five minutes later a jingle was aired, followed by non-stop music. At 18.06 Tommy Rivers told the station was back on the air after adjusting the antenna. He was heard till 19.56 and followed, up till 22.00 hrs by Liz West. Last one to be heard that day was Charlie Wolf for the final two hours. Of course, he had his own reasons again why the station wasn't heard for many hours:

"The real reason why we were off the air yesterday. What did everyone else tell you? Something about an antenna? Yeh, I thought they would yeah. Don't believe it, no. The truth of the matter is it was all done, it was my idea. I must take credit for it; Queen Mum was eighty-five years old yesterday. And I figured, you know – thank you – I figured, you know, would you want to subject your grandmother to US on her birthday. Silence is golden, that is my feeling."

Later on, in his show he was not so cheerful when he introduced a dedication: "This next song is a very special dedication; it's to all my very close friends, those of you in Britannia, o.k.? And all I can say is 'I'm sorry'. You don't know how sorry I am. Reflect on this, OK? Here's the Beatles with 'Let it be'. After the song he went on: "And once again to my friends: Sorry, that's not towards management. Management naff off!"

After saying goodnight and immediately before the closedown tape he suddenly decided to announce: "Laser 558, listen. Before we go, let's make it official: I might as well finally put it out. I'm leaving after this stint, I quit. This is my last trip out here because men can't live like this, OK? So, enjoy it while it lasts because next time I go on holiday it is permanent, OK? The TX was cut at 00.07 that night and listeners had something to think about.

On August 6th, more irregularity when Jonell started her breakfast program at 6.28. She took the mike till 10.28 when Erin took over till 14.00. Then we had Tommy Rivers till 16.57, while Liz followed till 20.00. Finally, for that day we had Charlie on air till 23.13. At the end of his program the complete deejay team joined him in the studio to do the chorus with 'Heartbreak Hotel' from Elvis Presley. At 23.14 the transmitter went off the air.

On the 7th we saw the same programming with Liz West presenting at 17.00 the Laser Chart Action. This time the transmitter went off at 23.16. On the 8th Tommy Rivers took thirty minutes extra, whereby Liz presented from 17.30 till 21.00. Then Charlie went on till 01.00, the normal closedown time for Laser 558. Charlie's depressed mood that he showed during the past days, had lifted by this evening. Rather talking about leaving the station he was talking about the possibilities of forming his own fan club – or rather 'appreciation society'. He got quite excited when talking about it.

During his program a helicopter started circling the radio ship, with searchlights on. Little did we realise that this marked the beginning of what was to become 'Euro Siege '85'. At 23.44 Charlie suddenly announced: "The transmitter is fixed, and we're now back to normal hours.'

The next day we saw a return of the 4 hour's slots with the same line up as on the 7th. It was the day we also learnt more about what was happening, although it was first on Radio Caroline where David Andrews told in his program: "I'd like to say hello to the official vessel that is anchored one hundred and fifty yard off our port bow of our ship." This and the previous helicopter mentioning on Laser learnt fans of both station that something was going on! Saturday the 9th the programmes were the same as on the previous day, except that Charlie was only on for one hour. It was time for Mary Turner and her syndicated interview programme, that week with David Lee Roth. After this we saw the return of Dr. Demento. On the Sunday we heard a new advert for 'Gridiron', a magazine devoted to American Football in the UK.

We learnt from Radio Caroline what the name of the ship, anchored nearby, was. On Saturday August the 10th, at 9.08 hrs BET it was Peter Philips who told listeners that it was the 'Dioptric Surveyor'. At first, we thought it was something of a tease between the two stations as Peter said the ship was leaving again after being there for at least 24 hours.

Indeed, the ship returned to the harbour of Harwich, but she didn't stay away for long! Johnny Lewis, who worked for Laser too, was on the Ross Revenge in those days and remembers: "It was on a Tuesday, August the 8th, that they passed us early in the morning, sailing south west to north east. I was on the air at the time. Obviously, they had been fitted out in London with all that sophisticated equipment and they went into Harwich, for supplies. The following morning, they came back and anchored less than three-hundred yards of our port side and stayed there all day and they were there all night too."

"Then on the Saturday morning, about 10 o'clock, they disappeared and sailed north-east and we never saw them back till the next Monday morning. For the first few days they were just sailing up and down the Knock Deep between us and Laser, arriving about eleven in the morning and disappearing about six in the evening. Then from about Tuesday in the second week they stayed all the time, just dropped anchor between the both of us, and stayed. There were always at least two DTI persons aboard. Normally they had, from what we could see, seven crew members. They were photographing anything that moved."

Laser's programmes were full of information about the crew members of the Dioptric during the following weeks. The ship was unstable and her crew members had been seasick. Johnny Lewis remembers: "They were anchored about half a mile away from us, because Laser and ourselves were only about a mile apart and they just anchored between the two of us. We were looking over there with glasses and just noticed that someone giving the old 'Huey' over the side! But it was very rough for them; we weren't worried."

Johnny Lewis

" Later they became a bit annoyed because the winter was setting in and I could think of better places to be on a smaller vessel than in the middle of the North Sea. Above that I couldn't think of anything worse than to be out there for almost a week doing nothing at all than watch the ships."

The next day the first of a series of commercials for the Sweeney Todd's chain of eating houses was heard on 558. A Laser Spot Song was also plugged: 'Mystery Lady' by Billy Ocean. Another way of plugging American football included the results on the Monday evening at 23.35 giving a credit for the information to Gridiron magazine."

Stewart Payne became an important reporter on the subject of Offshore Radio in those days and he was the first with a long article about the battle between Laser 558 and DTI. On August the 13th he wrote in the Daily Mail: "Britain's two pirate radio stations – Caroline and Laser 558 – were under siege last night by a Government chartered ship aimed at starving them into submission. In a major escalation of hostilities, the fast survey ship is under permanent patrol around the two vessels in an attempt to cut their lifeline of food, water and fuel supplies. All boats which go alongside the pirates at their North Sea anchorages off the Essex coast will be identified and photographed. They will be then intercepted by police launches if they return to British ports. Hired by the department of Trade, the patrol ship has powerful searchlights to prevent supplies arriving at night. Helicopters are also being used in the surveillance operation which is understood to cost around 50.000 Pounds a month. Caroline and Laser are not illegal because they are anchored in international waters."

Stewart was in contact with a spokesman of the DTI the day before and the guy confirmed that the 99 ft ocean going launch Dioptric Surveyor was on indefinite charter, equipped with highly sophisticated monitoring devices: "We will be keeping the Dioptric Surveyor on station in the Thames Estuary for the foreseeable future. We want Laser and Caroline off the air."

Stewart Payne was also in contact with the Caroline organisation and a spokesman had his opinion about the blockade: "This seems a massive waste of public money when all we do is provide a legal music service which is enjoyed by millions." He had contact too with a person within the Laser organisation: "They are trying to starve us out at enormous expense to the British tax-payer. But we will not give in. We will tender the ship from Spain which is not against the law".

Stuart went on with a conclusion of his own: 'The tough new moves reflect the growing alarm by legitimate British radio stations over the pirates' success. Both have powerful medium wave signals and have built up huge audiences – claimed to be ten millions – particularly in London and Eastern England.' Further on in his article, Stewart wrote about the big Caroline ship as well as the Communicator: "The Ross Revenge from Caroline is a veteran of the Cod Wars and has the greatest storage facilities. Both have large food freezers and storage for huge amount of tinned and dried food. But it is likely that both ships are low on supplies, including fresh water."

On the same day we found another article on the same subject in an edition of the Evening Star: "The Dioptric Surveyor, which today was in Harwich harbour taking on fresh water and fuel before resuming station by Caroline's converted trawler Ross Revenge and Laser's Communicator, is owned by Dioptric Ltd, a wholly owned subsidiary of Trinity House, and is on indefinite lease to the Department of Trade and Industry. A Trinity House Spokesman was unable to say how many crew were on board the operation, but it is equipped to sophisticated surveillance work, and was formerly owned by the City of London Polytechnic's School of Navigation as a radar training vessel."

Looking at the Lloyds Lists we learned that the former name of the vessel was 'Sir John Cass'. Further in the Evening Star on the 'Comments Column' we found another spot on the ship: "There comes a time in each government's life when it decides it ought to have a stab at getting rid of the pirate radio ships. That moment has arrived for Mrs. Thatcher's Government, but it will find, as all others have, that this is easier said than done. The pirates, despite little apparent advertising revenue, are great survivors. We suspect that the owners of both vessels will find new ways of servicing the needs of their ships and crews and that the current bid to starve them out will end, like most other attempts, in failure. Meanwhile the shore based radio stations are forced to compete with the pirate radio ships on unequal terms, for every record they play they must pay stiff needle-time costs, which are ignored by the pirates. In addition, the IBA demands that they schedule hours of talk programmes which seem to have a scant following. The best way to help local radio compete would be for the IBA to free its hands and not circumscribe it with petty-fogging demands which sounds splendid in theory but which make the battle sadly unequal."

In those days Ceefax and Oracle brought news on the 13th for the first time. Oracle had a rather unbelievable quote from a spokesman of the DTI: "Robbers of the airwaves are interfering with aeronautical and marine and navigation equipment, besides legitimate stations. Rescue helicopters might not be able to use their equipment in an emergency and Caroline and Laser were posing a grave potential treat to life."

TVS had a small report in their evening programme: 'The Government have launched a campaign to blockade the two pirate radio stations broadcasting from ships anchored off the Essex coast in International Waters. The Government, acting on request of the IBA and local commercial stations in Kent and Essex, has chartered a survey ship to keep watch on Radio Caroline and Laser 558. The aim of the blockade is to stop boats from British ports, mainly in Kent, from supplying and servicing the pirates. The crew of Radio Caroline claimed their supplies came from Spain – in fact both ships have been regularly serviced by boats from Ramsgate, Whitstable and Sheerness. The Dioptric Surveyor is on station to prevent any more comforts from English supermarkets reaching the ships.'

The newscast on TVS went on to tell viewers that the station was owned by an American Company from Connecticut and they interviewed Laser's General Manager, John Catlett. A summary of what he said: "Well it's a bit typically British to imagine that supplies and records, food and personnel could not come from other places besides Britain. We're prepared to go on broadcasting. We maintain that our American staff break no laws in International Waters. We want to go on serving these ten million listeners who are enjoying our programming, I think it's about, nine countries. It seems to me that if the British Government wants to spend what I understand is about fifty thousand pounds a week to watch us broadcast they're welcome to it; but I hardly think the British listeners want to pay the bill for that."

Meanwhile both Radio Caroline and Laser's staff on board the radio ships had reflected on the standing by of the survey vessel. On Caroline, for instance, special records were dedicated to the crew of the 'new neighbour' including one song with the lyric: 'Don't care if you just wanna hang around'. Also, the lads on board were invited for a tea aboard the Ross Revenge or to sample the notorious home brew GBH Bitter. On Laser 558 in the Liz West show there was some input from Beulah the Towelhead.

Liz: "Interesting question in that this one didn't come through the mail; this one came to us from a boat that's been boogieing around the Communicator over the past couple of days. The Dioptric Surveyor. Have you seen them out there?"

Beulah: "The little blue boat?"

Liz: "Yes, little blue boat, with official-looking flags, Anyway this apparently came from their captain. He sent it over this morning: "Dear Beulah, what to do about seasickness?" That's not really a silly question, kinda pertinent there"

Beulah: "Well it's not too cosmic but I could tell you – what is his name again?"

Liz: "It's Captain D.T.I. Beulah: They got no name?"

Liz:"   It's just initials, D.T.I., maybe: David Travers Inglestone', or something?"

Beulah: "If you're seasick there's nothing you can do, you have to have your heart into this operation. If you are just out here for fun and games you will be sick. That's it."

Liz: "   Is that why I never get sick."

Beulah: "We never get sick, because this is our life, but if your heart isn't into it you will get sick very quickly."

Liz: "So there's nothing you can do?"

Beulah: "Nothing. I'm sure they're all very sick."

Liz: "So they should just have a visit with Hughie and Ralph and forget about it?"

Beulah: "That's all they can do."

Who, we asked, are 'Hughie and Ralph'? We understand that it's an Australian slang expression for throwing up, and it soon became apparent that not everyone on the Dioptric Surveyor was a sailor. Some of them spent a lot of time 'studying the waves', as it was politely expressed on Radio Caroline. On Laser they used more drastic explanations and often seemed to take a perverse delight in the misfortune of the DTI monitors on the official blue boat, which soon became known as 'the Spy Boat'.

Chapter 17

EUROSIEGE '85

As an avid listener to the station at one point I used to turn on the radio daily when Charlie had started his daily reports from the quarter-deck on the progress of the Dioptric Surveyor, the government hired ship – which we saw as a spy ship. These special reports were heard for the first time in Charlie's show on August 14th, which is a remarkable day, since 1967, in the history on Offshore Radio. It marked the eighteenth anniversary of the Marine Offences Act.

In 1985 it was also the day that on BBC Radio One in their daily 'Newsbeat' Mike Partridge explained the details of the siege adding: "The department defends the costs of the operation, 50,000 Pounds a month, saying it has received complaints that pirate radio broadcasts have interfered with the radio distress frequencies at sea. And that could put people's life at risk.

Dioptric Surveyor

In those days Dilys Gane was a spokesperson for the DTI and she told the BBC: "Laser had a technical problem; their equipment wasn't working as they wanted it, and it jammed the distress and calling frequency. This meant that if somebody had an emergency at sea they wouldn't have been able to contact the land. Obviously, it's a thing which is constantly in the minds of the Coastguards, it's a nightmare for them."

Later we learned that several journalists had tried to get in contact with the Coastguards for more details, but that they had been ordered to answer with 'no comments'. Mike Partridge continued with: "The radio investigators say pirate broadcasts have also jammed messages to helicopter pilots; instead of vital information they got pop-music. Several times, particularly on the navigational aids, the helicopters are trying to land on the oil and gas installations in the North Sea; we have had to change the frequencies of the navigational aids because of actual danger."

Like in an earlier mentioned report once again Laser's John Catlett responded: "We selected the frequency specifically to make sure that we would avoid the possibility that we would interfere with any such air-sea rescue navigation frequencies or whatever. The possibility of freak propagation is always there for any radio or television signal, but the likelihood is extremely remote. It's an absolute waste of taxpayer's money."

At the end of August 14th Newsbeat on Radio One DTI's Miss Dilys Raines concluded: "It's our intention that they should know that we really mean business this time, and we certainly would prefer that they didn't starve, we'd prefer that they came in and gave up."

On the 15th Charlie Wolf played 'Laser Love' by the group 'After the Fire' and told us the deejays had adopted it as their station song.

Not all publications reported in an independent way. A reporter for the 'Star', Neil Wallis, wrote an interesting article, which was published on August 15th: "The swashbuckling Star sailed to the aid of Britain's beleaguered radio pirates yesterday. Po-faced men from the Ministry have mounted a blockade to starve them out, but we waived the rules to scupper the Whitehall Wallies, intent on forcing Radio Caroline and Laser 558 off the air. We loaded a fishing boat, aptly named the Freeward, with champagne, t-shirts, copies of Britain's favourite newspaper and other goodies and set sail at dawn.

Strict radio silence was observed as we battled through a force 7 gale to reach the ships moored a mile apart of the Essex coast."

" To nobody's surprise, the Department of Trade's blockade ship, the Dioptric Surveyor, was nowhere in sight. The SS Kiljoy apparently spends her nights locked up in Harwich and rarely arrives back on watch before noon. Somebody else obviously knew her sailing plans, for a supply ship was unloading fuel and provisions onto Laser 558. But it was the Star's cargo of fun that had the DJ's yo-ho-hoing with delight."

Petticoat Pirate Liz West whooped with joy when she got her hands on a Star T-shirt: "I needed a new one and this is just great!'. Grabbing a copy of the Star she cried: 'Wow, a newspaper; these are the first we've seen in two months. And it's a Star. Fantastic! It's the best for pop."

The crew then cracked open a bottle of bubbly to toast their 'absent friends' from the Ministry. Liz: "It's just like the Keystone Cops on the high seas.' Fellow deejay Erin Kelly broke off from broadcasting to the station's five million British listeners to say: 'It's hilarious. Fancy spending 50,000 Pounds a month to shut us down when all we're doing is giving a lot of kids a lot of fun."

After two hours of fun Neil Wallis and his colleagues left the Communicator and went back to shore and to their surprise the spy-ship came in view, just as they were leaving: 'She steamed to intercept us, but turned away when their captain had realised he had arrived too late. By this time the airwaves were rocking with the laughter of the DJs as they toasted their toothless watchdogs – with Star bubbly.'

Neil Wallis wasn't finished yet as the next day he had a follow-up article in the Star: "Clap 'em in irons! That was Whitehall's answer last night after the swash-buckling Star sailed to the aid of Britain's blockaded pop pirates. The Director of the Public Prosecutions was considering the same. And the men from the Department of Trade warned myself and other Star men involved:

"You face two years in jail, or unlimited fines. We are confident we can get you convicted. Five other vessels visiting these ships have been reported to police and will be investigated. The Star set out on a mission of fun to the pirate ships, but they were also trying to prove a strong point. Whatever spokesmen at Whitehall were saying the people at the Star were right. They proved that the spy ship was not in place in time to stop supplies getting through – and tit was in the public interest to prove it.

August 16th was 'Elvis Day' on Laser 558, in memory of the anniversary of his death. Songs from Elvis were interspersed liberally throughout all the programmes on that day. August 16th a record played a lot recently, was baptized by Tommy Rivers as the official Laser anthem song, being 'Laser Love' from the group 'After The Fire'. Erin Kelly gave special gymnastic exercises during her show for those on the 'spy ship'. Also, Laser used a temporary new name as the 'Freedom Radio Network'.

On August the 17th a BBC camera-team visited the Communicator and Liz West told us that the ship had also been buzzed by a light aircraft flown by Gary Newman and that he dipped his wings while passing Laser. During the day plugs were heard for the new Robert Plant album, while during the Mary Turner program in the evening he was interviewed. By the way, this program had commercials for 'Budweiser' and 'Levi's 501'. Some little gossip was noted too as we wrote down in our loggings that Mary Turner, whose shows were aired also on AFN and AFRTS stations was married at the time to John Catlett, one of the people at the New York office. And for another week Dr Demento was heard, the first time twice in a row on Saturdays, with sponsor Wrigleys Chewing Gum.

On August the 18th an article in the Sunday Times reflected that the DTI Patrol had also benefits for the radio stations in International Waters: ' The attempts to starve the pirates off the air have, however, given both stations unprecedented publicity which, according to Laser 558, a growing number of advertisers want to exploit. John Catlett, the General Manager said: 'We have initial conversations with a large number of advertisers who haven't been in touch before. Some of them are from categories that already advertise on the station, like record companies and movie houses. Others are in a new category."

If Catlett's claims were true the blockade appears to have given a much needed boost to Laser 558. The station, with overheads of around 35,000 Pounds a month, has few advertisers. The station's owner, a Panamanian company, recently gave warning that the station would have to survive in future by advertising revenue alone.

Despite the Panamanian base and the American style of Laser's operations, a Dublin entrepreneur, Philip Smyth, a hotel and disco-owner, is said to be the main investor. Catlett says: "some of the potential advertisers were British companies 'interested in trying to break this law, but we are trying to continue broadcasting on a basis as legal as possible. Trying to encourage somebody to break the law is not what we are here for."

On the 19th, Charlie informed us that they recently had a visit by David Chaney. He came out on one of the anorak boat trips to see them. After leaving Laser he was working on KMET in Los Angeles. During his stay on Laser 558 he produced a commercial for an LP, which could be ordered from an address in The Hague, the Netherlands. This was the P O Box from 'Haagse Harry' who was a mast climber and technician hired by the Caroline organisation. Several cheques arrived, but no LP was ever produced. Although the cheques were given to Chaney nothing was ever delivered to the listeners. When organising the Laser 558 reunion, in 2009, for the annual Amsterdam Radio Day, we tried to track him down to get back to Amsterdam but didn't find him.

The new Laser T-shirt, which was offered for the first time on August 19th, 1985, was of a very special design and obtainable only from the Laser Road show. They were printed with the expression: 'I spy for the DTI'.

BBC TV News also covered Laser in several news programmes on the 19th. They sent Gary Lloyd out to the international waters to cover the siege: "The Pirates call it Euro-Siege, they broadcast cheeky messages and dedications to the 'Men from the Ministry' aboard the surveillance vessel, that they call 'the spy ship'. The Department of Trade and Industry says it's not a blockade. They're keeping observation on comings and goings. They bristle with gadgetry. Since the Pirates are in international waters there's no power to prevent them broadcasting. The Ministry hopes to scupper the pirates through their suppliers. The DTI are convinced that some of their food and fuel comes from Britain."

Peter Phillips, in an interview on board the Ross Revenge, made the quote: 'We've been here for twenty-one years, I would think we will probably be here for a good twenty-one more.'

Regarding the earlier comment that a spokesman of the DTI called them 'robbers of the airwaves' Peter Phillips answered: "I've heard that suggested. They've also accused us of stealing listeners. Of course, but don't think listeners would agree that they've been stolen."

The BBC reporter went then to the Communicator arrived alongside in his little boat. Without asking any question he and his crew were greeted warmly by Charlie Wolf: 'Hi guys. Have you visited our spy-friends? They got anything to say for themselves? They are still throwing up? With a conclusion Gary Lloyd ended the news-item: 'However raffish 'on air' the pirates may have with their audience the Ministry say they're anarchists of the airwaves. They observe none of the regulations which control organizes stations. They pay no licence fee and in spite of the broadcaster's denials the Ministry say they're a potential danger for life!"

Almost each day television crews came out on small craft to visit the radio ships and to see how the Euro Siege was going on. On August 20th it was day eleven of the siege and, as well as the BBC, a freelance crew came out to do some shooting for ITN. Or they planned to.

Charlie Wolf reported live from deck on what actually happened: "We had some people out here shooting some film for ITN Television. Just as they were getting ready to start the interview, they were going to shoot up, from the side of their boat, their engine broke down. So, they tied up to our ship, and but they couldn't fix their engine. They got their emergency engine started and as they were pulling off, who pulls up but our good friends from the Essex Police Department. They chucked them a rope, and we're looking now on the horizon, just off to the west. They're now pulling this boat that had these guys are shooting some film for ITN, who they're now towing back into port. It's good to know that the Essex Police are out here doing their job. Tommy, and that's making the airwaves and the sea waves safe. When they were over here they had some guys shooting some pictures, both videos and 35 mil.'

Chapter 18

TV CREW ON THE HIGH SEAS

When reading the newspapers, we learned almost every day more about the British Governmental plans. It was August 21st that the London Standard had more: "An inquiry into pirate radio advertising has been ordered by the Director of Public Prosecutions. He has asked police to interview firms who have advertised with Radio Caroline and Radio Laser, who broadcasts from anchorages in the North Sea. The object of the inquiry is to discover if any offence had been committed by advertisers under the Marine Offences Act. Already representatives of a number of companies operating in London have been questioned. Officers are seeking to establish how advertising is paid for. The inquiry is made further complicated because some of the companies are American-owned. After the police report on the pirate advertising is complete it will be for the DPP, Sir Thomas Hetherington, to decide whether there are any grounds of prosecutions."

Talking about advertisers, on August 21st new ads and paid record promos were heard. First there was a commercial for a material arts catalogue. One was for a 'VHS Free at Home Demonstration'. Next was a record plug: 'Fifty Original Hits', available through the International Business Centre in London and a plug for 'Knock on wood', by Ami Stewart. That was not all, as there were also commercials for 'Courcy Champagne' and 'Seven Horses', a record by Icicle Works.

August 21st, at 21.01 it was told to the listeners that three or four hours previously they had moved to a new position. The MV Communicator had sailed ten miles to the north with the spy boat, the Dioptric Surveyor, in hot pursuit. Charlie told in his evening program about their new position: "It's true, it's amazing, we're about ten miles from where we used to broadcast from but it looks so different. Already I miss the Ross Revenge: you guys on the Ross Revenge, I'm going nuts! I'm staring out my porthole and they're not there. Of course, the Dioptric Surveyor is still there. It's a kind of a neat location because we're little closer to open seas and we're closer to the ferry lines."

"Hello to the guys on the 'Viking Voyager', who passed by a little while ago and we'll play a record for your guys later and also a record for the Sunk Pilot – and this is of course day thirteen of Eurosiege-85."

August 22nd brought a new advertisement for a country double LP available from the IBC as well as a promo for the Alvin Stardust Drive In Show. In Dutch newspaper 'Algemeen Dagblad' there was a short piece about the activities against Laser by the British DTI. The Dutch public prosecutor, Herr Wooldrik, was interviewed and told that no action could be expected in the near future from the Dutch authorities, although on the Ross Revenge there was also some Dutch people were working. All other action was, according to him, in hands from the British authorities"

A day later, on the 23rd around 14.13, Charlie broadcast a Eurosiege Update and mentioned that the radio ship was back on their former anchorage near the MV Ross Revenge. It seemed that they didn't have a particularly safe journey:

The Seawolf reported: "When we were getting up close to the Ross Revenge, the Dioptric Surveyor tried to overtake us and go between the two ships. I mean, you know, anoraks at heart, wanted to get the best pictures and I don't quite know what happened but I guess they got caught by a wave. It could have been a nasty accident if they weren't lucky, so I guess someone on the bridge over at the Dioptric was just a bit asleep at the wheel, but we're thankful that nothing happened to them because we wouldn't want to see any harm befall our friends there on the Dioptric Surveyor."

Some weeks later, while ashore, Charlie was asked by the Monitor crew why they decided to go back to the earlier anchor position: "I don't know, I really don't know what the deal was. I guess we were lonely. Part of it was that there was a big storm coming up and we were a bit lonely and we were not really in a protected area whereas in the Knock Deep we have sandbars on three sides protecting us. I wanted to stay out there until they spent big bucks and leased another boat; then we could have pulled back. It was just a wind-up more than anything else, Just to wind them up."

"And we gained the information wanted by moving and that is that they are more interested in us; because if anyone was going to get a delivery it would have been Caroline, because they were in the more protected area. And who's going to get a delivery on the High Seas? But they stayed with us, and left Caroline totally exposed to do whatever they wanted. So that showed to us exactly what was going on; with all deference to Caroline, had Laser not been there, had it just been Caroline, the Dioptric would have never been out there! They don't care about the Ross Revenge, but Laser being the very forward, frontal attack kind of go-getting radio station that it is, yeh that's scared people. So that's why the Government's out there."

"We show the IBA how it is done and the British don't like to be shown how to do it right. I don't think they're scared of propaganda. I can understand their argument; we could become a propaganda station, but we never have. The closest we've ever have come is the Euro siege thing and the only thing is that we're trying to protect our own buds out there. I've never got into politics over here; maybe once or twice I've made a comment."

He also comment about the fact that one day it was decided to go on regular times with the Euro siege updates, live from the deck as an outside broadcast: "I heard from a friend that they tried to listen at the BBC News Department for our up-dates but didn't know what time the next would come and so we decided for a regular time. Management was against this decision as I got a letter in which was mentioned not to do it anymore on regular time and also don't promote them on air. And me, being the irreverent person that I am, I did the opposite. Again, nasty letters from the management followed: 'Stop doing this, we mean it', but I figured everybody was tuning in. I was mad Laser wasn't selling commercial time; they could have sold the programmes, I thought".

And when talking to Monitor, the radio magazine, Seawolf also had some advice for some of the Independent Local Radio stations: "I hope that some of them like Eddie Blackwell would spend their money improving their own radio stations. The reason why we have the spy boat out there is because Essex Radio, Invicta Radio, Mercury are all losing listeners. And I can't understand what they're going through. But it's not Laser's fault. They're losing listeners because they're not providing what the people want to hear. If they could effectively nuke us off the face of the Earth tomorrow, nuke off Laser, Caroline, Sound East Sounds, JFM, Solar, Horizon, Nova, the whole lot of them, people are not going to tune in to Mercury, Invicta or Essex. Factual research has shown that a person will not tune in to what they don't want to hear. So instead of trying to get rid of Laser they should be improving their signal so people might say: "Oh, I'd rather tune in to Essex Radio any day than Radio Laser."

One day the weather worsened with the wind on the North Sea increasing up to force 8. The Dioptric left the Communicator at 16.00 hrs to shelter in Harwich harbour. That day also Mary Turner was logged, doing an interview with Phil Collins. In those days also new advertisements appeared on Laser 558, some of them fictional ones including 'Anorak DTI' offering an exclusive 'Laser and Caroline Together Forever' Poster.

Charlie came back on August 24th with more comments on the strange move of the Dioptric by saying: "It was a very unsafe manoeuvre for people at sea, as I've been told by our Skipper. They got caught in the tide and almost ended up banging into the Ross Revenge and, of course, we would have had to have rescued them. We would have been more than willing to because we feel we do have a responsibility to guard our little stretch of the ocean."

From Sunday August 25th more regularly Euro-Siege updates were heard at 13.15 and 17.15 BST. On August 26th, which went in the books as Day 18th of Euro siege '85' there were six deejays on the Communicator. That meant that programme hours changed again with Jonell from 05.00 – 08.30, followed by Erin Kelly till 12.00.Tommy Rivers was programmed till 15.00 and then Liz West came up till 18.00 hrs. The evening was filled by Charlie Wolf up till 21.30 which saw the return of Chris Carson till normal closedown time.

August 26th was the day that Charlie Wolfe did his major announcement: "Several days ago I have signed a letter of intent to join one of the ILR stations when I leave Laser Radio, and that should be when I leave for my next holiday, which is coming up, oh three weeks to a year you know, with the 'Moronic Surveyor' out there. But when I leave I'll be going to an ILR station and it's a kind of interesting deal, too because I'm going to start working for them while I'm here on Laser. I've actually sold them some time. It's like doubling up!"

Charlie then played a message from the managing director of Chipping Sodbury Sound, welcoming him to his new IBA station and its one hundred and fifty listeners. He added: "The only reason I'm going there is because not only do they pay me lots and lots of money, but they got really neat jingles, too."

He proceeded to introduce us to some of them – needless to say, they had been very carefully produced to sound as if the station was right up to date: for the nineteen twenties! These jingles became a regular feature of Charlie's programmes subsequently, as he explained he was also being simultaneously heard on Chipping Sodbury Sound via a satellite link.

Thursday August 25th Monitor magazine's editor Buster Pearson transcribed a detailed Euro-Siege Update: "This is day twenty-one of Euro-Siege '85. Charlie Wolf, reporting live. We've had a lot of activity up in the electronic monitoring room on the bridge of the MV Communicator and a buzz of activity in our situations room. I cannot see the Dioptric Surveyor right now. I can see the Ross Revenge; the reason is the Dioptric has changed its position. Instead of sitting between the two ships they're now sitting on our South side."

"They went there last night when they were chasing a punter who came by here and a very interesting situation came out of that. According to this guy, he had a visit from the Police a couple of days ago. The local constabulary asked questions, so these guys mean business. But they asked the guy what he was doing out here and he said: "Just taking pictures". He was not, I mean, even that guy, I mean he offered a fifty ton of fuel that he had on board his little small speedboat, but we wouldn't take it; but they mean business, they're asking questions."

"This punter asked us, he says: 'Listen, is it OK, is it illegal for me to even go on the ship? The police officer said: "No, it's perfectly legal, just as long as you don't bring any supplies."

"However, we're not letting anybody on board the ship, but you always can come by and visit us. Another interesting point we got from our electronic monitoring station in communicating with the Ross Revenge, they had an interesting talk with a fisherman on sea, here a couple of days ago. Now, as you know, they are always making the business of us being a potential life-threat, that's the DTI's claim that we interfere with the communications and distress channels. Well, according to this guy who's been on the seas for many years, he says he has never had any problems with his distress channels from any of the offshore radio stations."

It's already mentioned several times that the MV Ross Revenge was also transmitting from the international waters, anchored on a position in view of the people onboard the MV Communicator. It was Radio Caroline's third radio ship and came on the air in August 1983. As in earlier years, Caroline hadn't enough money to run the radio ship so once again, like in the days of Radio Mi Amigo, a Dutch organisation stepped in. It was December 1984 that Radio Monique started programming on the Ross Revenge. When the DTI was on the North Sea for a longer period with the Dioptric Surveyor, the news was on the radio in the Netherlands a few times.

August 25th the VOO, in their program 'De Grote Verwarring' (The Big Confusion) broadcast an interview. It was presented by Ron Bisschop, who worked as Johan Visser on the MV Mi Amigo. He interviewed Mr. Orie, a well-known expert in the field of international law. Ron asked him if there was any danger for the Dutch people on the Ross Revenge and Mr. Orie answered: 'There's nothing that the Ministry can do directly against the people on board the ship, including the Englishmen. As long as the ship lies outside the territorial waters and carries a flag that is not a British flag, the Ministry can't actually take any action on board the ship."

There still is the question, was he right with his conclusion? What if the ship had a Dutch registration? Surely action could then have been organised by the Ministry. Earlier, in 1981, the Dutch authorities had raided another offshore station, Radio Paradise, off the Dutch coast, carrying a Panamanian flag. Orie commented further on that circumstance: 'The High Council (in the Netherlands) has now ruled that such an action was illegal. The only point still to be decided is if Radio Paradise did at that time really fly the Panamanian flag."

Regarding the DTI action, Mr. Orie reflected with: 'Well, of course, if you have a boat near the radio ship you can check out who's visiting, what they do, if they take tapes on board or even bring out 'The Daily Mail'. You can see what they're doing on land and if the tendering with programme tapes, etc, is taking place from the mainland. According to the Strasbourg Treaty, assistance to a radio ship, has to be punishable by the countries concerned. So, if a Dutchman from Holland goes on board from a tiny boat from Scheveningen carrying tapes and sails in the direction of the radio ship, part of his activities take place in Dutch territorial waters, so can be seen as punishable."

On August 27th, 1985, Liz West finished her programme at 18.00 hrs and left the ship, probably together with Bealuah on the magic carpet, as he was not heard after Liz left. After doing her show till noon. Erin Kelly left the ship too. That Saturday, we also heard Mary Turner doing interviews with members of Power Station.

How did Tommy Rivers come up with the idea of 'Bealuah the Towelhead'? "Well, no-one has ever seen a picture of Beulah and he was this really cool guy. He came out to the ship because he knew that the kids out there could probably start crawling the walls after a month at sea. He was getting their minds tuned into the universe and, rumour has it, there was a character like Beulah on National Lampoon Radio Hour years before. Beulah enjoyed his stay out there and you can see his cover notes on 'I spy for the DTI' sleeve. Beulah has returned to a warehouse in Buffalo, NY, where he lives permanently, his mind in 1968!"

Let's see what happened on Friday August 30th, 1985. We had the radio on during late afternoon and it was mentioned that around 06.00 hrs the Dioptric Surveyor 'bugged off for a beer and a pretzel'. He said that a larger ship, the Farne, was standing by since 10.45 that morning. The real reason of the switch was not known but of course they joked about it on the radio stating that the Dioptric went back to harbour for emergency reasons. The hull was having a paint-job as they were scraping off the paint where the Laser jocks had put in the words 'Belgrano' and 'Rainbow Warrior'. Later, in the evening, the Dioptric Surveyor was back in near distance of the radio ships.

Figure 1Tommy 'What a Guy' Rivers

Chapter 19

DUTCH NAVY TO ASSIST

On September 3rd, in bad weather with 'near storm' force winds (Force 9) he Dioptric Surveyor left her anchorage to seek a safe place in the harbour of Margate. It's not sure, but it was suggested by Charlie Wolf that the boat was dragging her anchor. Soon after the Dioptric left, the Dutch minesweeper M857 with the name the Makkum, circled the MV Communicator and anchored near the MV Ross Revenge.

Comments were made in Laser's programme: "Does a minesweeper carry any armaments? That's we want to know before I start taking the Micky out of them." Instead of doing so, Charlie Wolf used a Dutch phrase book to refresh his knowledge of the Dutch language. Charlie seemed quite worried until he was assured the 'Makkum' really was on a mine sweeping exercise, especially when a Dutch naval helicopter also arrived on the scene. Two days later the Dutch navy vessel left, early in the morning. Not much later the Dioptric arrived back in international waters which Charlie led to: "This morning the Dioptric Surveyor, after being gone for about 36 hours, showed up at the scene and I yelled to them: "You guys are back? You must be kind of bored, seriously, just sitting there, doing nothing all day", and the guy said: "well no, we listen to you!"

Johnny Lewis recalls the time the minesweeper was out there, doing exercises in the neighbourhood of both radio ships: "Around six o'clock in the morning one of the people on the Ross Revenge mentioned it to me that a Dutch navy vessel was circling us. I thought: 'O. my God' and I go up seeing that they were just waving to us. They sailed about half a mile north east of us, then suddenly all these green and red lights came on. Black marker buoys went up, and from my knowledge of the sea I knew that it meant that they were minesweeping. They put rubber boats in the water and were probing here, there and everywhere. So, we called them up just to say: "We can see that you're minesweeping, when you sweep past us can you watch our anchor chain?" It was just to find out what they were up to.

Their skipper came on and said: "Yeh, Ross Revenge, and no problems at all, we do know about your anchor chain, hope everything is okay with you. We can see you've got some friends out there from the British Authorities."

We replied with: "Yeh, they keep an eye on us; are you doing the same for the Dutch Authorities? He then replied that the MV Makkum was just a training ship and even asked for some request, to play. There were four older people on the bridge and for the rest about twenty young guys just to learn the job."

September 4th we learned that the Laser programming was shortened as they started at 06.00 and closedown was at midnight bringing it to a total of 18 hours a day. It was Broadcast Magazine in which 'We're not interfering' says Laser' was published in the edition September 5th: 'Radio Laser has sent an open letter from New York to Home Secretary Norman Tebbit challenging them to provide evidence of Laser's alleged interference with marine and air navigation equipment and emergency communication. "If these statements are true then I wish to place on record that it is scandalously irresponsible of DTI inspectors not to have contacted us immediately so that we might make any adjustments to prevent this interference", said Laser's General Manager John Catlett.

"Our engineering experts do not believe the DTI statements to be true. We regard the latest action as simply as a response to the vociferous lobbying of the British commercial radio stations who are anxious to protect their absolute monopoly." The DTI said it has had complaints about interference with navigational equipment particularly in the Harwich area. The Civil Aviation Authority has reported interference with automatic direction-finding equipment on board helicopters approaching North Sea rigs. A CAA spokesman said this could lead to bearing errors which could be dangerous at night or in fog.'

On September 7th Hall and Oates were interviewed in the Mary Turner's program. The Sunday the 8th brought a very late start of the station as Jonell didn't commence her programme until 8.45. And this was the day we all had been waiting for. As mentioned earlier the studio clock brought the wrong time and that Sunday the clock had been put right! At 12.00 Jonell was followed by Tommy Rivers. Three hours later Chris Carson took over till 18.30. Then Charlie Wolf came on the air, very subdued, and he made very few announcements.

Mysteriously that day he called his programme 'the three loaves of bread show' and signed of at 22.02 using the name 'Rick Stevens'. Charlie told in his report that he had contact by the radio channels with the captain of the MV Grey Echo, a tugboat which was working for Trinity House. The captain told him he had never heard about complaints that Laser was interfering with emergency frequencies. Scott Shannon was heard next till closedown with the Top 30.

Monday September the 9th we heard again some new commercials. First herd was 'ZX Offer', a herbal dieting course. Next we logged 'Kimstar Fashion Jewellery', 'Three men on a bicycle expedition', which was a charity ride in Australia also sponsored by Laser 558. Also, a UK Tour for Gary Numan was promoted as well as a song promo for 'We all want to be in love' by John Wilson. Charlie Wolf started his programme at 19.30 in the evening again with the new name for the show, using his own deejay name. He told us: "I'm giving you a boring show tonight. It's what the management wants". Later he came back with: "You won't hear anymore Euro siege reports, because we just don't care anymore."

Johnny Lewis recalls the Euro siege period: "Well Laser made a big thing of Euro siege, we on Radio Caroline played it our way but not cool as some may think. I think that we have answered the allegations of interference. I don't think we should have done all the Mickey-taking bit, but at the same time, credits to Charlie for what he has done. He's brought out the fact that something stupid was happening out there and they were just wasting money. And he has made it sound like it was all fun, so I think he did a good job. But as far as Caroline is concerned, I wouldn't like for us to have done it! But we agreed on the Ross Revenge it was all great, brilliant. We were listening to Laser every night. There was no telly on between nine and one o'clock. Everybody was listening to Charlie and we were just killing ourselves laughing. I don't think there was anybody on Caroline who could have put it across as well as Charlie. It was good fun at the time, and it was good fun for people to listen to."

On the 10th, that month, there was contact again with the New York office and one of the subjects was the plan to erect a higher mast before the winter would start. The idea was to combine the two transmitters aboard and so to strengthen the power to 40 kW. The idea, however, was never materialized. Another rumoured idea was the plan to take one specific sponsor for the weekly countdown on

Laser 558. A company interested would get 60 spots a week in conjunction with the promo for the show and the price for that would be 4800 dollars a week. Two days later, September 12th there was another new commercial for King Style, a fashion chain.

Laser's John Catlett told us that he would fly to Texas to interview three people for new deejay jobs. On September 13th some changes in staff as Craig Novack was back on air between 05.00 and 09.00 o'clock. As there were, with Craig's arrival, five jocks on the ship, four hours shows were reintroduced. From 09.00 – 13.00 Jonell, followed by Tommy Rivers. From 17.00 till 21.00 Chris Carson followed, with Charlie up till closedown time at 01.00 BST. That same day five new record promos were noticed: Black Lace with 'I speak da lingo', Warren Mills with 'Sunshine', 'Let me hold you closer' sung by the Jamaica Boys, Kevin Kitchen and 'Fingerprints' an finally 'State of the heart' by Rick Springfield.

It was now Day 36 of Euro Siege '85 and Charlie gave his last report from the poop deck of the Communicator, meanwhile filmed by a crew of East Anglian Productions. Charlie: "I survey the scene and I don't see the Surveyor, the Moronic Surveyor. It left earlier today, buggered off in bad weather. The coast is clear at this time. Tommy, from what I have understood, we had a boat come by,'Grey Echo' and the guys waved at us and they were sure nice. And from what we understand the Moronic Surveyor should come back soon. We'll go up to the electronic monitoring station on the bridge of the Communicator and check the scene out there." Tommy Rivers added: "And they picked up their spy mail too Charlie." He responded with: "We want to thank everybody that's been writing to the boys on the spy-boat and you can still send in more letters and what we may do is deliver them to Fleet Street in the future. But they did get their first shipment of mail today." The conversation went on for some minutes on the same subject ending with the comment that it was a very boring day."

Saturday September 14th brought some maintenance time for the transmitters and so the station was off the air from 10.00 in the morning, returning some 30 minutes later with a carrier, followed within 3 minutes by the station opener, normally heard in the early morning: 'From the MV Communicator in International Waters we are Laser 558, owned by Eurad SA, this is free radio with non-stop hit music, practicing good programming and technical standards. We are Laser 558.'

As it was a Saturday the syndicated programmes by Mary Turner and Dr. Demento were expected but we didn't hear them at all. The Sunday had the syndicated programme 'Rockin' America Top 30' with Scott Shannon between 22.00 till 0.45.

On Monday September 16th, 1985 the UK Press Gazette had another article on Laser and more: "The war on radio pirates is intensifying and all around the British coast the Department of Trade and Industry is putting up notices warning boat owners of the consequences of supplying goods or carrying people to the pirate broadcasting ships. The two main pirates are Laser 558 and Radio Caroline, which are both outside Britain's territorial waters, so the DTI can only restrict their operations by prosecuting British nationals who supply them with food, advertising and technical assistance."

"Under the Marine Etc. Broadcasting Offences Act 1967 convictions can lead up to two years imprisonment and heavy fines. The Director of Public Prosecutions must first approve before a case is brought and already he is considering the papers dealing with an alleged attempt by reporter Neil Wallis of the Star newspaper to take out champagne and gourmet food to the pirates. Photographic evidence was taken by observers on the Trinity House vessel Dioptric Surveyor which keeps pirate broadcasting ships under surveillance about 15 miles off the Essex Coast.'

Monday the 16th brought a very early tender to the radio ship and this day went into history as the day that Jonell, Charlie Wolf and Tommy Rivers left the Communicator for the very last time, leaving only two presenters on board. From 06.00 till 12.00 we heard Craig Novack live. He was followed by a program till 14.30, from when nonstop music was played with an odd announcement here and there from Jonell (taped earlier). The same thing happened with the voice of Tommy Rivers until 1600, when Chris Carson then followed live up till 22.05. She was followed for the next two hours by a nonstop tape, now and then interrupted by Charlie's voice. Closedown that night was at 00.05 hrs. The next day was slightly the same but was also the last day that programmes from Charlie and Tommy were aired on Laser 558. That day we heard some new ads: for Admail in London, the Sandown Salver horse-race and a CTV offer.

'Regal Rock and Blues Competition' was the name for a new competition which started on September the 18th. The winner of this competition was invited later for a weekend in London, including a big rock and roll revival show in The Albert Hall with artists like Chuck Berry, Bobby Vee, Bo Didley and Dell Shannon. This day between 12 and 13 we heard Jonell's voice for the last time doing voice overs in a 'nonstop' show and then between 19.05 and closedown time at midnight, a new deejay, Jay Mack from Boston.

September 18th also brought Laser back in the newspapers as the next was published in the London Standard, to be precise in Peter Holt's column 'Ad Lib': 'The future of North Sea pirate radio station Laser 558 looks distinctly bleak. This week five disc jockeys have quit in a dispute over pay and conditions and the station has been forced to switch to pre-recorded tapes. Charlie Wolf and Tommy Rivers, the remaining original deejays from the team of ten who began broadcasting in May last year, jumped ship last Monday night. They hitched a lift to Ramsgate on an English fishing boat. Three other jocks on shore leave have also resigned. All five, staying under aliases in London, are waiting for Laser's American managing director John Catlett to return from a DJ recruitment drive in the States. Wolf, who claims he is being constantly followed by Department of Trade and Industry Investigators, says: "There are only two deejays left on board and they've had to start playing recorded tapes. I've had enough. Morale on board has been very low and the food has been terrible. I'm owed quite a bit in back pay and can't afford to leave London until I've got it. I'm really sad about quitting. Laser is a great station but it doesn't seem to be able to generate enough cash to survive."

September 19th was divided into six hours programmes with Craig Novack back on board between 06.00 and 12.00, followed by Chris Carson. Jay Mack was heard between 18.00 and 24.00 hrs.

On the 20th of September again the London Standard brought attention to Laser in Peter Holt's column: 'The Department of Trade and Industry's blockade of the North Sea pirate station Laser 558 appears to be working. Laser's ship, the MV Communicator, has been unable to take on supplies of fresh water for the five past weeks – a direct result of the DTI monitoring vessel moored nearby. "It's horrible", says DJ Tommy Rivers, who is back in London and returns to America next week to finish a degree course in communications research at Minnesota University. "None of us has been able to wash and it's been particularly tough on the girls." Rivers says the next two months are crucial if Laser is to survive. "The first task is to get replacement DJ's from America. If they can keep going for a couple of months they'll survive the blockade. The sea becomes very choppy in October and the DTI will have to retire."

On the 22nd, as it was a Sunday, Scott Shannon was scheduled but absent and so Jay Mack continued until closedown. The telephone connection with the New York office taught us that day that soon, a new deejay, Chuck Cannon, would arrive on the ship. On the 23rd Craig announced that the 'I spy for the DTI' record wouldn't be in the shops that day as the release was planned a week later. The same day a new record promo was heard for 'I want to be a cowboy' by the band Boys Don't Cry.

On the 25th of September programming changed again with Craig from 06.00 12.00, Jay Mack till 14.00, 14.00 – 20.00 Chris Carson, including 'The Laser Chart Action' and from 20.00 – 24.00 Jay Mack again. During his program Jay announced that 'Laser would be off the air for the next few days due to essential generator repairs.' The next day, however, transmitter and generator were switched on again between 19.38 and 24.00 and brought us Jay Mack behind the mike.

Late September there were rumours that the British authorities were planning to get in contact with the Panamanian authorities to get the official registration of both radio ships withdrawn. To get more information we contacted the Central Shipping Registration Office from Panama in New York and asked the shipping consultant Julio Chanson if the ships were still registered and he promised to look into the case and come back to us. When getting back to the Freewave office he said that two months earlier, a procedure began to withdraw both registrations. He wouldn't confirm whether the procedure had been started after requests from the British authorities or if the organisations behind Caroline and Laser hadn't paid the annual registration bill. He simply said: "Call back in three weeks, maybe I can tell you more." He added that both representatives of Laser and Caroline in Panama had already been informed about the plans to withdraw the registrations.

When Tom de Munck called Glenn Kolk, Laser's attorney, he promised to get in contact with the New York registration office. After a discussion with Julio Chanson, he reported that in early October, both registrations could possibly be withdrawn. John Catlett from the Laser organisation, after being informed by Tom, was very surprised to hear that no one except the Freewave Media Magazine, had taken contact with Julio Chanson and asked himself what the hell Kolk was doing.

On September 27th programme schedule was the same as on the 19th, so back to six hours slots. September 27th was also the 50th day for Euro–Siege '85. There was a remarkable moment in the Chris Carson show. She played 'London is the place for me' we remembered so well from Big L and she asked the listeners if they knew which station used the jingle, way back in the sixties. A day later several comments were made in Laser's programmes, from which we learned that a top up of the food supply was urgently needed. A new record promo for 'Love take over' by Five Star was heard for the first time that day and a tender arrived during the day, as from 20.00 – 01.00 newcomer Chuck Cannon was on the air for the first time. He told listeners that he originally came from San Francisco in California. On September 29th we heard Scott Shannon again, after a week's absence. His show went on till 0.45 after which Laser 558 closed down for that Sunday.

The 30th September saw the same programming as on the 28th of September and that remained for the next four days. 'Burning Questions' by the Korgies was another record promo we heard on the last day of September. It was also the day that former Laser deejay Jessie Brandon became part of the team at Radio Nova in Ireland as the Home Office were making it impossible for her to obtain a work permit, which was necessary to work for Capital Radio in London.

In 2010 I asked Jessie how she became involved in Capital Radio: 'The news of the Capital Radio job offer either came in a radio call from New York or an in-person visit by John Catlett, I forget. Capital Radio had contacted them. Knowing how money-hungry the people at the New York office were, I'm betting money changed hands to get me out of my contract. John Catlett has told me he felt so sorry for us on the Communicator; our mail was held up and our pay checks were always too little too late, while the New York sales staff took trips to Las Vegas! I was told to pack and take a meeting with Jo Sandilands at Capital Radio. I had no idea what salary was appropriate, so I took what they offered. My choice of dollars instead of pounds delighted them, I had no idea what the exchange rate was. But the pay started immediately, regardless of their success or lack of success in getting me a work permit.

I was paid while on a vacation in the US and then they set me up in a Times Square hotel to do a Saturday show by satellite from the studios at KISS-FM and tape Sunday's show. They flew over people from London to produce the show. They flew back almost immediately with the Sunday tape."

"I remember their Music Director, Tony Hale, was there for the first set of shows. He held up a sign from the other side of the glass – "Laugh, damn it! That's what we hired you for!" After Tony it was Jon Myer who produced the program, while the last series in New York were produced by Duncan Meehan. Then I got the OK to do just one show a week in Britain, for six months, after which time they denied my work permit entirely and I went to work for Chris Cary's Radio Nova, on Declan's recommendation.

Jessie Brandon

Chapter 20

MORE AND MORE REPORTS

We had been missing them weeks but October 1st Laser brought them back into the programming, the Communicator Club Numbers and instead of LP records for the winners there were free copies of 'Music Master''. The same day we heard a new commercial for 'Starmaker', which was an agency for pop groups with a telephone number in Chelmsford.

On October 2nd we discovered that Tommy Rivers had decided not to return to the radio ship and to look for another job in radio in Great Britain. A day later Charlie Wolf appeared again in the London Standard in a small item: 'Laser's 558 little joke with their adversaries at the DTI continues. Last week Laser jock Charlie Wolf was outside the Department's Waterloo office making a video for the pirate radio station's single 'I spy for the DTI'. "I was skulking by a wall when I heard someone calling my name. I looked up and a person was hanging out of a fourth floor window taking my photograph. Big Brother, or just childish? Laser fans do get everywhere, you know.'

On the 2nd we also learned that the ship's auxiliary generator was running. Chris Carson presented the Laser Chart Action and then at 20.42 Chuck Cannon spoke about a helicopter flying around and shining its spotlight onto the ship.

A day later ,a personal copy of the 'I spy for the DTI' was received and on the cover we found, among others, the following sleeve notes: 'Recorded at CIA International Studios – Washington D.C. Engineered by Bill 'Vodka' Voigt. Additional Lyrics by Ted the Cowboy, Scott Budweiser, Beulah the Towelhead and Susan Lindsey Botheltrob. On the front cover beautiful colour photos of the MV Communicator as well as the Dioptric Surveyor.

From the 4th of October Laser was off the air again. No official reason was given when we contacted the office but an oil shortage could have been the reason. However, a day later it was confirmed that again damage occurred to the antenna system during the storm on the 4th. The station was back on the air on the 8th of that month. We heard that Chris Carson left the ship to take a break and a newcomer was John Leeds.

The three DJs took six hours programmes each during the 18 hours a day broadcasts with Craig Novack from 06.00 till 12.00, followed by Jay Mack and at 18.00 Chuck Cannon. We had to go back to February 2nd, 1985 to find a complete male line up on Laser 558 again. That day also brought a new commercial for 'Computer Inside', with an address mentioned in Penge. Also 'Car Date' and a plug for the Motor Fair '85, to be held at Earls Court in London, were heard.

A day later programming was back to five hours with the arrival of John Leeds. On the 10th we heard a new record promo for 'I'll be your friend', by Precious Wilson. On the 11th Craig completed his programme and John Leeds took over at 10.00, but the station suffered, from what we believed, a generator failure at 12.09 BST and Laser was silent for the rest of the day and the following Saturday October 12th.

The Ipswich Evening Star of October 11th announced that Euro siege was continuing: 'Radio ships in North Sea will continue to be watched by DTI Investigators for the foreseeable future. The Department's ship, Dioptric Surveyor, will remain anchored near Radios Caroline and Laser until all those who have supplied the vessels have been identified said a spokesman: "We have no plans to leave the area".

On October 12th the Melody Maker brought more about the four persons leaving the MV Communicator: 'Charlie Wolf insists that the deejay's exodus was purely coincidental. He also denied suggestions that money, or lack of it, was the reason for his departure. "It was a lot of resignations at once", said Laser's General Manager John Catlett, "but you have to expect this kind of thing when you're running an offshore radio station. Liz West found that conditions were difficult with us, and her resignation was a surprise although I fully understand that she came to a point where she decided Laser was not for her. Jonell only signed with us for two months and she's got a radio job to go to in the USA. Charlie Wolf's resignation came to us as a surprise although he had given some warnings."

Sunday the 13th it was a late start as the transmitter was switched on at 3 minutes to eight in the morning, but from that point it was 'Sixties Sunday' again with the Laser deejays up till 22.00 hrs, when the syndicated Scott Shannon 'Rocking America Top 30' followed till closedown. As Scott was on holiday, the show was presented by Shadoe Stevens.

October 14th the Ipswich Evening Star quoted the Minister responsible for the Euro Siege: 'Technology Minister Geoffrey Pattie has dubbed the pirates, who have thousands of Suffolk fans, as 'potential killers'. He insisted: "We are not spoilsports who are against pop music but this has greater importance than listening to Duran Duran." The DTI had now had enough and been made very unhappy the way publicity was given to their Euro siege, especially as it was costing so much money and had no apparent effect at the time."

That same day I got a telex from one of the contact persons I had in England in which a success for the authorities was mentioned as a court case had taken place in Southend on Sea. Three persons appeared in court due to the fact they had trespassed the Marine Offences Act 1967. Donald Hill, Howard Beer and Graham Bushell had to pay a 500 Pounds fine as well 20 Pounds costs. They were arrested on March 8th doing some tendering in international waters.

Another new deejay came aboard from Missouri, Jeff Davis, which brought programmes back to four hour slots and total hours of twenty a day. At 13.00 it was the debut for Jeff. During his show he told listeners that he came from St. Louis but had been working in radio during the recent seven years in Arizona, only 50 kilometres away from the Mexican border. He came to work in the North Sea to be away from the rocks and the cactus. It seemed Jeff had really problems during his first show as a lot of flies were tempering his enthusiasm. At 11.30 we heard John Leeds mentioning that Her Majesty was circling the Laser ship and that moment can go into the Laser history as the last time that we heard one of the team referring to the DTI. The next four days brought no changes in programming.

More than 25 years after Jeff Davis stepped aboard the MV Communicator I had contact with him and asked him where his roots were and he told me: "I grew up in St. Louis, Missouri and at 17 years of age I entered the Broadcast Center of St. Louis." Of course, I wanted to know more and so I asked where he worked in radio more before going to Europe: "Prior to my graduation of high school and the Broadcast Center my parents moved to Tucson, Arizona. After graduating I joined them in April of '78 and got my first job in radio in May at 93.7 KRQ. I turned 18 just 2 months earlier. I was working 10pm to 2am at KRQ when I left for Laser 558 in September of 1985".

I was interested to know how he came to work for Laser 558 and Jeff told me: "At KRQ I worked with Blake Williams. He was a part time

DJ who had an engineering licence. He heard about Laser early on and joined Laser before it launched. A year later he returned and shared his stories and photos. The timing couldn't have been better as I was looking for a new venture. Blake's interesting tales intrigued me. He told me they were looking for new talent so I took the opportunity to send a demo tape.

To my surprise the general manager, John Catlett called me one day to see if I was still interested. I told him I was and we arranged to meet in the Phoenix airport one afternoon to discuss it. After hearing his description of the situation, it sounded appealing enough to me that I agreed to accept his offer on the spot."

What was his first impression? He came with a very interesting answer: "I flew from Tucson to Newark, New Jersey and met up with another new hire, John Leeds. His real name was Chuck, forget his last name. He had to change it as we already had Chuck Cannon on air, and we flew to Gatwick airport together. We were in separate lines in Customs."

"When I got up to the podium they changed agents on me. The new agent was asking a series of questions including how much money I had on me. I said two thousand dollars, though I only had about $100 since I was going directly to the ship, and he asked to see it. I thought I was being clever by saying it was in my luggage to which he replied "Let's go get it." I knew I was sunk so on the way to baggage claim I told him the truth; I was arriving to work on Laser, I was getting on a train to the coast then on a boat to the ship and I'd be out of the country in a matter of hours. That didn't matter to him. They went through every piece of luggage I had then locked me in a little room. I tried to track down more money by phone hoping that would satisfy them but the decision had already been made to deport me. Ugh! Three hours later, I was on a plane back across the Atlantic. I stayed with a friend in New Jersey for a few days while the company arranged to have me fly to Amsterdam."

"When I arrived there, I was hooked up with some of the folks who provided supplies to the Ross Revenge. The couple I stayed with in the Netherlands was Leen Vingerling and his partner Marjo. They were gracious enough to take me in as a guest for that 11 day period. We've remained in touch ever since. At that time, the remnants of a hurricane was traveling down the Western European coast. The seas were too rough for the tug to head out to the ships. Finally, 11 days later, we drove several hours to the Belgium port of Nieuwpoort, boarded a tug with a group of Anoraks and eight hours later we arrived at the Ross Revenge. I was instructed to pretend to be an anorak as well. They did not want the others to know they were delivering a DJ to Laser. It was a pleasure to have the opportunity to see Radio Caroline and the Dutch station Radio Monique.

After the visit, and exchange of supplies, we rode over to the MV Communicator and Laser 558. I distinctly remember as we approached that rusty old ship thinking "What the hell have I done?" It was hard to imagine what the next year would bring. Little did I know it would only last just over a month? John had no trouble getting through customs at Gatwick airport. By the time I finally arrived, he had been on board for two weeks! The anoraks were quite surprised when the rope ladder was tossed over the side and I climbed up! After meeting everyone on Laser I immediately felt at ease and was looking forward to my new adventure. I was hired to work the 1 to 5pm shift."

Next the question of an official contract signed before working for the station? "When I met with John Catlett in Phoenix I signed a year contract. The appeal was that I would work six weeks then get two weeks off. I could tour Europe or head home. I couldn't wait to take advantage of that opportunity. However, it never really happened."

On October 16th a TVS crew with Alan Clark visited to the Communicator to make a short item, with Jay Mack being interviewed:

Jay: "You can tell everybody we have no intention of leaving."

Alan: "You reckon, you're gonna be there for some time?"

Jay: "You bet. We hope; we know! We're having a great time out here. We love it! It's too bad that the DTI isn't having any fun!"

In order to justify its continuing, the DTI took to the road on October 16th to explain to hand-picked media representatives why they're so desperate to force the offshore stations off the air.

In an unusual press conference staged at Hollingbourne, a DTI spokesman, Peter Anderson said: "We are bringing the anti-piracy war to the pirates' own backyard to tell the public what a nuisance they cause. They are cocking a snook at regulations with their massive transmitters and giving a tremendous headache to all radio users. We have to stop them, otherwise we will see anarchy of the airwaves in this country as the radio stations with the biggest transmitters' hijack audiences. We want to drive home to suppliers of the vessels, many of whom live in this area, that the Government takes a very grave view of their actions and will seek prosecution under the 1967 Marine Broadcasting Act."

Those attending the Press Briefing heard yet again the numerous stories about the pirates and interferences on official frequencies and official figures were given to as from the day the Euro siege officially started, the DTI had recorded ships visiting the pirate radio ships and had counted 17 vessels, including one hired by a national newspaper which sent a reporter to the ships. John Catlett, Laser's general manager – was quoted by John Nurden in his article as responding: "I don't want people to go to jail simply because they want to do business with us, but we are a commercial venture and if it becomes unprofitable we would probably not continue."

At the Press Briefing or conference, there were three officials from the DTI who tried to produce technical evidence to support their claims that Laser and Caroline were a serious threat to air and sea navigation in the Thames Estuary, English Channel and the North Sea oil-rigs, pop music from the ships interfered with navigational beacons and this could cause accidents and loss of life.

DTI officer Dilys Gane claimed: "It's a very serious threat. The pirate radios are putting out such power that they are jamming both the frequencies they are using, obviously, and surrounding frequencies. We have had numerous complaints from helicopter pilots trying to land on oil rigs in the North Sea because their directional beacons are being jammed by the pirate radio ships. And instead of getting the signals to help them to land in those very dangerous conditions they're getting pop music. These stations are completely uncontrolled and, for example, last year they blocked out the navigational aid at the entrance to the English Channel, the busiest sea route in the whole world, and therefore, for a period of hours, if there had been any emergency, the Coastguards wouldn't have known about it."

The officials claimed that they couldn't rule out the possibility of towing both ships into port if the blockade failed and mentioned that such a decision had to be made at the highest Governmental level.

Let's see what the editorial comment in the Ipswich Evening Star on October 17th, 1985 had as a subject: 'If there is clear evidence that their broadcasts are endangering life and causing major headaches for the emergency services and legitimate shipping that could then dramatically alter their image. So far, of course, all we have heard is accusations but little proof, and one wonders why if the facts are there, the Government hasn't decided to use this most potent weapon instead of the impotent 'cat and mouse' strategy which seems to achieving very little. The pop pirates have been around for two decades steadily building up their image as loveable rogues. A blistering broadside aimed at their image – showing them to be heartless parasites endangering human life, if that is what they are – might be a far better strategy than the current one."

Jeff Davis reported about the tenders which were boarded by the authorities: "As the government was stopping supply boat captains, our deliveries became less frequent. There was a period when we went nearly two weeks without water. I recall getting just enough water out of my cabin sink to wash my hair twice during that period. Thankfully, we never ran out of beer or food. "

Mentioning the Corona Foundation, I remembered my own visit to the Communicator in 1985 and thought of refreshing memories from Leen Vingerling, the organiser, along with Rob Olthof, of many trips with Anoraks to the radio ships in international waters during the mid-eighties. I asked him when these trips to the ships had started, from where and what was taken out to the radio ships.

Leen: 'The tendering of the MV Communicator was more of secondary importance. We were the most important supplier of Ross Revenge and after this ship was tendered with water, diesel and food, we passed by the Communicator. The Laser organisation had their own suppliers, the Murrays from Sheerness and, if I remember well, they had also sometimes a big tug, which was tendering them and which came from Southampton."

"The Laser organisation did not want a tender company, that also worked for their competitor, Radio Caroline," explains Leen. "So, we didn't supply the Communicator with basic essentials, things like food, fuel and water. We took sometimes crew and deejays to and from the ship, and sometimes small equipment parts for the studio as well as the machine room."

"My contacts with people on the Communicator started in 1984 when making some trips with Anoraks," Leen remembers: "At first we were not allowed on the Laser ship but after a few months this changed. The crew on the Communicator thought it was time to see other faces for a while than those living on the radio ship and also liked to be in contact with those who intensively listened to their programs. In those early months of Laser 558, Captain Tim Levensaler was there, living like a hermit and suddenly he gave permission to come on board. Thus, he acted in disregard of the orders of the New York Office. Tim was the second helmsman during the voyage from the USA to Europe and was second captain next to Captain Boucher."

"It happened very coincidently when there were some personal problems on the Ross Revenge so that we were not allowed to step aboard. And so, the deck of our tender was filled with crates of beer and all kind of sweets like egg cakes, raised cakes, filled cakes and more from the bakery 'Brothers Tetteroo'. Originally meant to go to the Ross Revenge but all these things now went to those aboard the Communicator helping to break the ice very fast. Later the crew on the Communicator informed their office that our big tender, the 'Zeemeeuw', could also be hired for tendering the MV Communicator completely.'

During those many visits, to the radio ships, Leen and his skippers sometimes found people were unsatisfied: 'On one of our travels we took the Communicator's engineer Bill Voigt back to shore and so he stepped from the tender onto the harbour of Nieuwpoort, in Belgium. The organisation behind Laser 558 let him down and although they promised to replace him, nobody appeared. Bill wanted to go ashore and asked me to take him back ashore. He was the cousin of actor Jon Voigt and came with us to Nieuwpoort and then on to Oostende. From there he took the ferry to England, making it a very long travel to arrive in England.'

I also asked Leen Vingerling how the relationship was with those on the Communicator: "The Americans were very hospitable and also very interested in the behaviour of the Europeans. The Anoraks, we took to the North Sea, always brought along some food and drinks for those on the radio ships and that became our permit to come aboard. They really enjoyed seeing us again. It's a relationship we built step by step. At the Laser's office in New York, they had the rule that no one may visit the ship. In reality, it was different and I could guarantee them that we did not have anyone on the tender with bad thoughts. However, with most of the people on the ship I couldn't build a very good relationship as it was a dovecote of persons. Every time we came back to the Communicator there were new faces.'

Leen Vingerling & Captain Willy on the tender Windy,

I asked Leen whether those who were involved in tendering the ships were paid for it: "For bringing people to the ships or taking persons off the Communicator, like Bill Voigt, David Chaney, Jeff Davis, Erin Kelly, Jonell, Mike Barrington and others, we were not paid," said Leen. "This was of secondary importance. As the MV Communicator was anchored very near to the Ross Revenge we saw this as a favour. Next to that, one good turn deserves the other and so visits from Anoraks to the Communicator were also guaranteed in that way"

Next I asked Leen Vingerling if he ever had the idea that the authorities were at his neck and he confirmed: "Yes that was during the period of the spy ship when the Dioptric Surveyor was anchored close to the Communicator. Also, we got the impression from our home harbour of Nieuwpoort that, at one stage, there was more pressure. A few men who seemed a bit aggressive appeared on the quayside. Everyone knew them, wearing leather jackets and sunshades. When we had tendered the Communicator one day, we were followed by the Dioptric Surveyor for more than an hour and I must say that this was an impressive demonstration of power."

Was there ever direct contact with the top of Laser 558? "Well, when those regularly tendering the Communicator stopped doing so, I got a desperate John Catlett on the phone from London asking if we would do the complete tendering for the organisation. This was no problem for us, but I asked for payment in advance. This wasn't possible for him, as the money had to come from the USA. Next we heard, a desperate appeal was made as almost all the diesel had gone from the tanks aboard the Communicator. I knew this form of 'humanitarian emergency call' so well from the Caroline organisation and had no intention to fall for it. Complete tendering wasn't offered by us as a result, and John Catlett broke down in tears.'

The last question for Leen Vingerling was if he remembered any nice anecdotes: "Well, the one which comes up directly is the trip we made with anoraks, including Eduard van Loon, the chairman of the Caroline Radio Club in the Netherlands. At one stage, when not too far away from the Communicator, he went to his cabin and reappeared in a beautiful three piece suit. He wanted to look impressive and was delighted to see the ladies on board. He even took flowers with him. Of course, this expensive suit was later filled with green algae spots for when he had to climb the rope ladder he slipped and didn't look quite so impressive!"

Regarding another incident, this time with the dinghy. Jeff Davis recalls: "One afternoon a few of us decided to give the dingy a workout and take it over to the Ross Revenge. We used the crane to lift it off the deck and place it in the water. I don't remember who was in the group, but there were about four of us. After a bit of effort, we got the motor running and were on our way. We only made it about a quarter of a mile when the motor gave out. A first we weren't too concerned but after several failed attempts to get the engine running, we realised the gravity of the situation as we started drifting. We were heading toward the MV Communicator but to the aft of the ship. If we didn't get help we would drift out to sea. We started yelling for help and got the attention of one, then two of our shipmates. An attempt to throw us the line fell short. We were getting closer aft. One more attempt made it to the dingy. Just as we reached the aft of the ship, we were able to pull ourselves to the side. Sure, some passing ship may have rescued us but who knows how long and how far we may have drifted before that would have happened. Of all days that was one when the DTI was not in sight. Though, I wonder if they had rescued us if they would have been able to detain us Americans and deport us rather than returning us to the ship'.

Jeff Davis also remembers some heavy storms on the North Sea: 'A storm was brewing late in October. Our captain received reports that this was going to have gale force winds. There was concern that the winds would push the ship, dragging the anchor, toward a sand bar just a mile or so behind us. It was determined that each of us would work a shift to assist the captain if needed. The captain had to run the engine at several knots to maintain our position and not drift backwards.

I had the midnight shift. It was quite an experience riding out the storm on the bridge with the captain. It was intense but I don't recall feeling much fear over the situation. Then came a request from the Captain; he asked me to take a flashlight down to the bow of the ship and lean over to determine the anchor chain's angled to get a better idea of the direction we were facing. I'm not sure why the compass wouldn't have helped but it wasn't my place to question him. I gathered up my nerve, buttoned up my coat and with flashlight in hand made my way down to the deck. The wind and rain were beating down. The rain soaked deck was so slippery it felt like walking on oil. It didn't take long before I took a spill. Having played sports most of my life I had good balance but I hit the deck hard. I slowly made my way to the starboard bow. As with most ships, the bow leans outward so I had to bend over the top of the bow to get sight of the anchor chain below me. What a rush it gave me to have the waves crashing in on me. I was soaked, feeling a bit reticent yet full of adrenaline. That was the worst of it for me. I believe my shift ended at 4 or 5. The captain maintained control throughout the early hours until the storm blew over, later that morning.'

Liz West was interviewed by a TVS crew in Rochester, where she was staying in the Gordon Hotel. The interview was shown on the 23rd October during the news magazine program 'Coast to Coast'.

The introduction to the interview was done by Cathy Alexander: "An American deejay claims the pirate ship Radio Laser has abandoned her in Kent owing her several thousand pounds. Liz West describes conditions on board the ship as 'horrendous'. The crew, she says, often wait for weeks with hardly any food. Liz West is one of seven disc-jockeys to leave this year. It's believed that all are owed money, but Miss West is the first to talk openly about the station's problems:

Alan: Liz West, a 24 years old radio-announcer from Palm Springs, California, claims she has been left high and dry in Rochester by pop pirates who failed to honour her contract. She was hired by Laser's General Manager John Catlett in California in January. She was then offered thousands dollar a year and went on board Laser 558 on February 13th. After a trip to New York last month to negotiate record company deals for Laser she returned to the Hotel in Rochester which the station uses to accommodate staff on their way to the radio ship. She says, when she was asked for her pay, she was told she was sacked. Apart from a two weeks holiday in Morocco, Liz West says she's spent seven months working for Laser but has received no pay, only hotel expenses.

Liz: "Well I'm owed two-hundred-and-two-days. Including my holiday time, it works out to be around six thousand dollars; whatever the rate of conversion is today, I don't know, but somewhere in the area of forty-five hundred Pounds. What Laser is doing is they're taking the money that they're giving me in order to eat et cetera; they're taking that out of the total sum that they owe me.

Alan: So how much money do you actually have to your name right now?

Liz: About twenty pence.

Alan: Seriously?

Liz: Seriously.

Alan: You're saying you're destitute?

Liz: Absolutely.

Alan: Do you have a contract? Can't you take any legal action?

Liz: The contract was drawn up in Miami and the company is based in Panama, so it's a Panamanian corporation supposedly; so, if we wanted to take them to court we would have to do it in Miami or Panama.

Alan: Can I ask you about your time on board the Radio Laser ship? You were on for some very long period, weren't you?

Liz: My first turn on the ship, I stayed out there for fourteen weeks. It was basically on my own volition so I really can't blame Laser's management for that one; although this last stint out there, which was in excess of ten weeks, I had tried desperately to get off the vessel because of my health, because of I had health problems stemming from a bout of dysentery. The station really made no effort to get me off.

Alan: In what way were the conditions on board horrendous?

Liz: No fuel, no water. The women on board, myself included, went without feminine hygiene products for two months; the food – when I left – was down to I think half a bag of pork chops and a package of bacon, there were no fresh vegetables, there was no milk. The Captain on the vessel thought I had scurvy because I hadn't had fresh vegetables for so long. I had broken out in what were hives, or resembled hives. And it's basically a mess. There was no toilet paper anymore, it was just bad. I'd gotten to the point now where I just want to write this off. I mean much of it has been a grand adventure but it's also caused me a lot of trouble. I'm disappointed and saddened and I'm hurt by the fact that I feel that what I've done for Laser warrants some respect and I haven't gotten it, at least not from Laser's management.

Alan: No. It's been suggested to me that you're giving details of the Laser's operation to the DTI. Is that true? If so, why?

Liz: I've been approached as have been many people within the organization. They've been approached, Charlie Wolf's been approached by the DTI. We are not at this time prepared for details because we're hoping that things will sort themselves out, that we will get taken care of and that maybe this project has a future.

Alan: How much longer are you going to stay in this hotel in Rochester?

Liz: Well, until I can't afford to do it any longer. And then I don't know what I'm gonna do.

Alan: Laser's general manager, John Catlett, claimed today Liz West had resigned. He said it was true that they owed her money but only about fifteen hundred pounds. He also admitted Laser owes 'substantial amounts' to a number of former employees.

On Monday October 28th, after waiting for more than a week, Laser 558 returned to the air at 06.00 BST with Craig Novak in the chair up till Midday. He mentioned that 'Baddie Boat' was anchored close to them and at 10.53 he even said 'hello' to the Essex Police boat which was also nearby. Then 3 hours with Jeff Davis followed. Jay Mack presented between 15.00 and 18.00. John Leeds was next to 21.00 and the last slot for that day was filled by Chuck Cannon till 01.00. One new record promo was heard for the LP 'The best of Jethro Tull'.

The next day hadthe same DJ order, with 4 hour shows from 05.00 till 01.00 , a schedule that remained for the rest of the month of October. To our surprise, new commercials were heard for: Pleasure Box Fashion Fair, Bleeper Key Ring, Starfighter digital watches, a home security firm, a curtain and carpet cleaning service and a Hi Fi Unit. Most were sold direct from the International Business Centre at Mortimer Street in London. The final hour of Jeff Davis, between 20.00 and 21.00 was called 'The Happy Hour'.

October 29th is was the Guardian which brought us new plans by the authorities to end Radio Caroline and Laser: 'The government is to try to put the two main floating pirate radio stations, Laser and Caroline, out of business by persuading the Panamanian authorities to withdraw registrations of their ships. A Foreign Office spokesman said that it would approach the Panamanians if requested by the department. Without the protection of the Panama flag the ships would be breaking the International and British law requiring all large commercial ships to bear the flag of a sovereign nation. If Panama withdrew the registration it would take the companies some weeks to register the ships in another country to which the government could make the same request.

Both the Communicator and the Ross Revenge are believed to have expired safety certificates. The Panama Bureau of Shipping inspected the Communicator nearly two years ago, but has not inspected the Ross Revenge, which British investigators believe has a transmission aerial which does not comply with international construction standards.'

On the 30th in Laser Chart Action show we learned that 'I spy for the DTI' reached the number fourteen position that week and the same day Buster Pearson read in the Southend Evening Echo, more about the song: 'The record is proving a hit in Southend's record shops, like 'Our Price' , 'Parrot' and 'Golden Disc', where it has been on sale for the past week. The record included the words 'hundred thousand bucks a month to bring Laser to its knees'.

'The Southend Evening Echo report added that Laser was back on Monday morning after a nine- day loss of transmission due to generator problems.

Paul Rusling told me that I Spy for the DTI was recorded in London by Paul Young and a Manchester band Sad Café, with extra vocals by Laser's Robbie Day and two of the Laserettes. It was released on the Farce label, but despite good sales did not appear on the charts.

In his program on the 31st Craig Novack played a song recorded by two listeners called Roger King and Yanni Tsamplakos. It was called "Laser Radio" but did not get released until January 1987, so missed on lots of promotion and was not a hit.

Chapter 21

ACCOMPANIED BY A SISTER-SHIP

Listening to Radio Caroline early on November 1st, 1985, the breakfast DJ Nick Richards, told us that he couldn't believe his eyes and thought he was seeing double. When he looked in the direction of the MV Communicator he saw also an almost identical ship anchored next to the Laser vessel. Late the previous evening, the DTI had replaced the Dioptric Surveyor with a bigger vessel, the 443 ton MV Gardline Tracker.

The Gardline Tracker had been a sister ship to the Communicator, and was also built in 1953 by Abeking and Rasmussen in Lemwerder, Germany. In 1985 the ship was owned by Gardline Shipping Ltd. and registered in Lowestoft.

On Laser 558, remarks were made on air that morning by Jay Mack: "A beautiful boat, because it looks just like ours. You look out there and you think you're looking in the mirror or something – same colour. Nice bright orange, same design. I think it's a little shorter. I don't know, they haven't given us any measurements yet, but it's a nice looking boat."

The newspaper Ipswich Evening Star was the first to mention it in their pages on that same day: 'There will be no love lost when two sisters meet on the high seas as the Government's crackdown on pop pirates takes an ironic new twist now the Department has hired a larger and more stable ship, the 443 ton Gardline Tracker, the sister ship to Radio Laser. "Monitoring boats supplying the two radio ships had been highly successful and will continue through the winter", a DTI spokesman said today.'

November 2nd a new commercial was heard for a Fashion Fair as well as for another compilation album from Jethro Tull. The programme on November 2nd started only at 07.00 and due the late start Chuck Cannon decided to extend his show till 02.00 the following morning.

The newspapers had also something to say that day as the Daily Mail reported that Laser was almost bankrupt, which was followed on Sunday November the 3rd by the Mail on Sunday, which included lines like: "In the early days of heady success when Laser went on the air on May 24 last year, it had a proper New York office. But today it is based at 9/1 Kensington High Street in London, where it hides behind the name 'Overseas Media Inc.' This is an American registered company claiming to be an agency placing clients' advertisements in the best outlets, but nearly all these commercials go to Laser."

"The most controversial aspect of Laser's advertising is what it calls 'Spotlight Records' – and what others call payola. They were the idea of Robbie Day, the Englishman in charge of drumming up advertising for the flagging station. And how they work can be described by disc jockey Liz West, 24 from Chicago, until recently Laser's music director: "For a lump sum of 5.300 dollars a record company would get 14 plays of the song per week and also 21 commercials, each 30 seconds long, for the record."

There were fierce protests from the young staff, and it was agreed that two brief disclaimers would be put out each day admitting that Spotlight Records were a form of advertising. "We were all aware what this would do to our careers, but eventually we went along with it because we saw it as the only way we would ever get paid", said Liz. Laser boss Catlett admitted that most of Laser's revenue came from this type of advertising and said: "I'm perfectly satisfied that what we are doing is legally and morally correct." Catlett was also manager of OMI. He claimed doggedly that the station really does have an office in New York, manned by part-time staff. But he admitted that almost all the advertisements handled by OMI have been placed with Laser. And Liz West said of OMI: "It's a front, it's Laser's London office."

We can reveal that a series of meetings with the giant Philip Morris industrial group took place in Switzerland, and Laser was confidently expecting several hundred thousand pounds of advertising for Marlboro cigarettes and 7-Up. But as Glen Kolk, then the Miami-based lawyer for Laser said: "The deal fell through and in characteristic fashion, Laser went ahead and ran advertisements for Marlboro." Philip Morris was astonished and made a comment: "Whatever they have put out has been broadcast without our authority".

Advertising man, Robbie Day, had, in the late seventies and early 1980, also been working for the Caroline Road Show. He came from

Beckenham and in 1985 was a director of Laser Roadshow Ltd, a UK registered company, which was running road shows in England and being heavily advertised on Laser 558.

In the earlier mentioned interview by Chris Edwards, Tommy Rivers was asked about the land based support, from people like Robbie Day. "Robbie had been on the air on Radio Caroline and then he started doing sales for them at some stage of the game. He surfaced a few months after Laser came on the air. We hadn't got the pan-European advertisers that we hoped for and the big Marlboro deal had fallen apar. This meant that we had to hustle and do deals."

"That was right up Robbie's alley, with record companies etc. He worked out of at least two offices in London. Back in those days, our lawyer said it was supposedly legal to go out and solicit business in London. We had to, in theory, fly the clients back to New York, sign the contracts there, because it made it legal, then fly them back. You'd have to check with Robbie if he ever actually did that! He has always been a wheeler and a dealer and Robbie is actually a fun guy to be around but don't ever lend Robbie a fiver because you'll never see it again."

"Robb Eden was there too and was more of a straight shooter and he was a great guy with a young family at that time. He was doing some sales for us and Caroline. One of his deals was Arabian Sands; Liz and I went out there for a week or two and Robbie and Nikki came out for a week and we had a good time. We've been in touch over the years as well and Robb has always been a friend."

On November 4th something was happening; although nothing was mentioned on Laser, there were some remarks made by Susan Charles on Radio Caroline about "their friends on the Communicator taking their vessel for a sail around!" At 22.00 hours Scott Shannon's syndicate programme was aired for the very last time.

That day, an incident happened when nine members of the Free Radio Association and two crew members of a cruiser got frightened. They planned to visit both radio ships during the weekend. When they arrived near the Ross Revenge two rubber dinghies were lowered from the Gardline Tracker and went straight to the cruiser.

The following day, a spokesman of the FRA told a reporter from the Colchester Gazette that it was a panic situation for a while. After arriving back on shore, he made a complaint to the DTI about the incident.

Another incident happened the following day, on November 5 was reported on BBC TV's 'Look East': 'Essex Police and Customs officers have questioned four crew members of a fishing boat at Harwich. The crew of the 'Windy' called for assistance when the vessel broke down near Radio Caroline ship.' The Windy was a Honduran registered vessel manned by Dutchmen and usually captained by Willy Wrury.

On the evening of November 4th, the Windy was immobilised by a rope fouling its propeller while sailing between the Communicator and the Ross Revenge. The Walton on the Naze lifeboat was called out and towed the Windy to shore. Once the green-hulled Windy had arrived in Harwich, the crew was interviewed but the police had no reason to arrest them on any charge. They were ready to depart from Harwich's Trinity House Pier in the evening of November 6th when another ship sailed past, the MV Communicator!

Before that momentous voyage into port, we heard Laser 558 for a only short part of November 5th. Craig Novack was on air between 05.00 and 09.00. The first sign of trouble came at 08.14 that Monday morning when Craig asked the management to contact the ship: "This is a message for those who are interested. All Yankee Three are Zero. Uniform, repeat Uniform, November, repeat November, Romeo, repeat Romeo. Channel 16 listening. That's the message. We'll repeat this every 15 minutes, interesting hey?"

At 08.30 more coded messages were given out for someone to contact them in 15 minutes time on Channel 16. The sarcasm clearly demonstrated that the crew was disgruntled, but we didn't know how serious the problems were. Craig was followed by John Leeds. During his program the station went off the air at 12.21 after the song 'We're ready for the world' was played. Well, this song was not the best choice to be played at that stage. When the music was ceased the transmitter stayed on for just one more minute and was switched off for the final time on Laser 558. The main General Motors generator, which powered the transmitting equipment, had completely failed and the Lister generator, used for running ancillary services, was also malfunctioning.

At a later stage we heard that there had been intense contact between Captain Paternoster, aboard the MV Communicator, and Caroline's engineer and then captain Mike Barrington. All sources to produce electricity had almost failed and only the ships lights could be on at very low power. Mike Barrington, tried to give Paternoster much good advice, but sadly in vain.

On Caroline they listened a lot to the radio channels and even heard John Leeds asking the Coast Guard from Walton on the Naze to get him off the Communicator, which was refused. The atmosphere was quoted to us as being very depressing. They had used the last few gallons of freshwater to cool the generator.

In the radio contacts between the Communicator and Mike Barrington on the Ross Revenge, Captain Paternoster threatened several times that he wanted to get the Communicator into harbour 'as soon as possible'. Barrington informed him that a tender, with spare parts, was on the way but Paternoster responded that he didn't believe it as so many things had been promised and never materialized.

When talking to one of the Radio Monique deejays, the sister station on the Ross Revenge, we learned that Captain Paternoster had already warned his crew and the DJs that he would bring the ship into harbour. Anoraks visiting the ship were informed by him that he was very dissatisfied in the way the tendering and payment were done and he was planning to bring the ship into a Dutch harbour soon.

That Wednesday, November 6th, we heard the news on Radio Monique, Radio Caroline's sister station. In their news at 11.57 Dutch time, they broadcast a special news summary, repeated on Radio Caroline by David Andrews: "The offshore radio ship MV Communicator, home of Laser 558, sailed from the Knock Deep Channel today, escorted by the British Government's surveillance vessel 'Gardline Tracker'. The Communicator had been plagued by generator problems since yesterday and, after a night of heavy storms on the North Sea, the Government vessel took up position alongside the ship earlier today. It isn't yet known if the Communicator had asked for assistance or if the authorities boarded the vessel. Both ships are now believed to be heading for Harwich on the east coast of England. The crew on the Gardline Tracker would not comment on whether or not the action they had taken was done with the authorization of land-based officials." He then handed the microphone to Andy Johnson to give a look back at Laser's time on the North Sea.

"Laser 558 was one of the most successful offshore radio stations to challenge Europe's land-based broadcasters since the first of such stations took to the High Seas in 1958. Its programmes of non-stop hit music at one time had an audience of eight million listeners. But from the time Laser arrived off the East Coast of England until today the station was plagued with technical problems".

Then a summary of Laser's life followed. Andy added: "Nevertheless the station was seen as such a threat by Britain's local radio operators, who found their listeners deserting them in droves to the brash, American newcomer, that they put press on the British Government to silence both Laser and their neighbour Caroline. The Government surveillance vessel took up station in the Knock Deep Channel of the North Sea, where both ships are anchored. The Authorities claimed both ships were supplied from England, in contravention of legislation passed in 1967 to silence offshore radio for once and for all. In fact, both Caroline and Laser tendered from Spain. Last night's storms, coupled with a lack of cash and ever increasing generator problems, finally proved too much and Laser's brave attempt to shake up European broadcasting came to an end. It is ironical that the Government's ship 'Gardline Tracker', which escorted Laser to Harwich, was once upon a time a sister-ship to the Communicator."

Susan Charles also talked about the MV Communicator leaving the area: 'Station Planet Earth is closing down; transmissions end; from all of us here at the Caroline Organisation, our best wishes and all our love to everyone at Laser.'

Anglia TV broadcast the news at 13.25: "We've just heard that the motor vessel Communicator, which houses the pop pirates Radio Laser, is on its way to Harwich harbour. The vessel will be met by officials from the Department of Trade and Industry, customs officers and the Essex Police. The news came from the government spy ship, Gardline Tracker, which has been monitoring both Radio Laser and Radio Caroline in an attempt to starve them out. Conditions on board are reported as appalling, and disc jockeys and crew say they cannot cope any longer with shortage of fuel, water and food."

At dusk the Communicator arrived safely in the river Stour and sailed serenely past the Trinity House private pier, which Trinity House had very kindly opened up for the media camera teams and the Free Radio Supporters. Several hundreds of them had arrived to watch her sail in. The Communicator went on to settle down for the night off the Parkstone Quay; at that point, no-one left the ship.

During the TV Programme 'About Anglia', which was aired early in the evening, we learned that it was the captain of the Communicator, Patrick Paternoster, who asked in an SOS for assistance for him and his crew. His reason was that the circumstances on the ship got worse and worse and there was a complete power failure. He was concerned that the ship would start taking in water during the forecast force nine gale and there wasn't sufficient power to run the pumps. When the anchor was raised, a pilot was put aboard the Communicator and the ship was accompanied by the sister ship Gardline Tracker and a vessel of the Essex Police. She had lost her immunity with the captain's decision to go into harbour.

Later we learned, that earlier on, help was offered by the crew of the Gardline Tracker but this was refused by Captain Paternoster. As a result, the Communicator's crew and DJs spent several very unpleasant hours bobbing around like a cork in the high winds. When the offer was made a second time by the Captain of the Gardline Tracker, Paternoster, supported by most of the crew onboard the Communicator, accepted. There wasn't enough power to raise the main anchor, so crew of the Gardline Tracker helped to cut the chain.

Let's go back to Jeff Davis his memories about the last days in the life of Laser 558: 'Over a short period of time we lost five of our six generators. One morning one of our engines threw a rod. It was one of the loudest noises of colliding metal I have ever heard. We had to hand pump oil into the engine for hours. Each of us took turns pumping the lever up and down over and over again. When we were down to our last generator with no parts scheduled to arrive, the captain felt he had no choice but to head to port. If that last generator had failed we would be dead in the water. You may recall the coverage of our 'surrender' on television. There were police boats, DTI personnel, and helicopters following us all the way into Harwich

Port. The plan was to appear to be giving up with the intent to secure parts and get right back out. When we arrived there, Customs agents boarded the ship and searched with their drug sniffing dogs. Nothing was found. When they were done, they asked for each of our autographs!'

'News at Nine', the BBC TV main evening bulletin, had footage of the floating reception committee awaiting the radio ship: "A phalanx of police and customs men set off for the ship to interview the disc jockeys and crew. It seems that on Laser tonight they'll have to face the music of a different kind as the investigators try to find out who did what."

It was still on November the 6th, the most hectic day in Laser 558's history when the 'Eastern Daily Press' disclosed news of complaints by the Gardline Company: 'Survey firm Gardline claims it is owed 5,000 Pounds in the wake of a transatlantic deal connected with the trendy radio station. Two years ago, the company sold the former survey ship Gardline Seeker to an American organisation. Shortly afterwards, the vessel turned up off the Essex coast, as the MV Communicator, from which the radio station operated. Gardline plans dramatic action to recover its money. In true nautical fashion it intends to have a writ slapped to the mast of the vessel.

Gardline spokesman Mr. Darling explained that the ship was bought through a Swiss law firm, Ivan Cohen & Co. of Geneva, to Deka Overseas Inc, based at classy address on Madison Avenue, New York. At the last minute Gardline was asked to deliver the vessel to Florida. Payment for the ship was made at Barclay's Bank, Mile End Road, London. After the 25-day crossing, independent shipping broker, Mr. Paul Hodge, paid with two cheques to Gardline. The money was to cover additional fuel and labour charges incurred in the crossing and the cost of installing a satellite receiver on board. The cheques were stopped and according to Darling, Gardline claimed that it was owed a further 1408 Pounds. In its efforts to recover the sum, the company discovered that Deka Overseas Inc. was nothing more than a brass plate company – literally a brass plate and mailing address on the door of a New York lawyer's office.

Darling said: "We have been as nice as we can and they don't dispute that the money is owed. For a long time, I've thought that the sum won't be recovered. The hassle over the Gardline Seeker , or the Communicator as she is now known, wasn't purely a business problem as it also intruded in my family life. My three sons listened to the station as did my daughter Melanie. She thinks that her father is trying to chase Laser!"

The Thursday November 7th edition of the Daily Express ran an article with the header: 'Pop pirates must face the music'. It was written by Eileen McDonald and was a report on what happened a day earlier with the Communicator: 'A pop pirate radio ship limped into port yesterday after surrendering to men from the ministry. Radio Laser 558 had gone off the air when the generator on its North Sea ship blew up. A spy boat hired by the Trade Department offered help – on condition the pirate crew accepted its escort into Harwich Harbour, Essex. At first the outlaws refused. But after 24 hours they thought the Communicator was in danger of sinking in a force nine gale, so they gave up. Unrest on board caused by an outbreak of food poisoning and scurvy also helped to prompt the surrender decision. The Communicator was led to within a mile of the coast by the Government vessel, which had been monitoring the pirates and preventing supplies reaching their ship.'

In the Daily Mail, a reporter wrote that the captain had also asked for assistance by the police as he thought he might be attacked by the DJs. On arrival in Harwich, those on board the radio ship were in danger from the authorities. A spokesman of the Essex Police had some good news later on: 'We will be making inquiries to see if any offences have been made, but at none of the crew appeared to be UK nationals, so we do not think there will be any charges.'

In the news programme 'Coast to Coast' that same evening Buster Pearson heard reporter Ray Rogers telling: "There were eleven people on board when she anchored seven Americans and four Britons. They have all been questioned but at this stage there's no suggestion of any charge. The four Britons are still onboard."

On the quayside in Harwich was John Catlett, Laser's manager, who was interviewed by Rogers and here some of the quotes he made:

John: "I'm going out to visit the vessel and I expect that the American disc jockeys will be coming on to land."

Ray: "But you're going out in a police launch, is that significant?"

John: They offered me a trip and I accepted.

Ray: Are the police questioning you? John: They haven't so far. They were very pleasant with us last night and offered us rides in several directions.

Ray: Can you tell me what the future for your station is?

John: I can't tell you the future.

Indeed, Catlett was seen by other people on the quayside making urgent phone calls from a telephone box. He said that he had visited the ship and that there had been neither a mutiny nor any case of disease, as had been reported. He also confirmed that it was no trouble for him to get on the ship and was confident that this wouldn't change.

The story spread quickly that crew and DJs were anxious to get their money and when asked about this Catlett said: "There was no such demand when I visited them last night and about the future, I can only tell you that it looks grim. It doesn't look as good as it did three days ago."

Final team: Craig Novack, Chuck Cannon, Jay Mack, John Leeds and Jeff Davis

November 7th is a day that Jeff Davis also remembers: "The next day we met with the Immigration official. After giving us a 30 day visa, rather gracious considering we were enemies of the government, he asked for our autographs."

"It was an ironically humorous experience," says Jeff. "We stayed in a hotel in Rochester in Kent for two weeks hoping to get the opportunity to get back out. It never happened and sadly, we were provided with tickets to head home."

On November 8th the 'Daily Mirror' commented on the end of Laser 558: 'Almost the only people who are pleased about the pirate radio station Laser 558 going off the air are the spoilsports of the Department of Trade. The station gave pleasure to millions. But pleasure was not the yardstick by which the Department's inspectors judged it. They were determined to close it down. Now they are after the only remaining pirate station, Radio Caroline. They claim that they are only upholding the law. The Marine Offences Act bans pirate radio stations. The law would force those who want to listen to popular music to tune into BBC's Radio One or licenced commercial radio."

"Wouldn't it be better to sit in silence than to listen to mock- cheerful, self-opinionated, self-important smugness of most Radio One deejays? BBC Radio One was only created because the early pirate radio stations were so popular. They couldn't beat them that way, so they tried to drive them out with the law. The continued mass appeal of stations, like Laser and Caroline, shows that the public wants them. Is it too much to ask from a Government that claims to be a supporter of competition of free enterprise that it should stop wasting taxpayers' money in hounding those who give so much pleasure?'

In another TV item that night in 'Look East', the BBC's news magazine for East Anglia, Charlie Wolf was interviewed. He was at the quayside too and told viewers: 'I spoke to Laser's general manager and he told me that things were looking good. There was food on board, but they were running out of water, but we've run out of water before. I think one of the problems is you've got to remember is, that it's a relatively all new crew. The disc jockeys are all new and they're never gone through some of this stuff. Now, when I first came on yeah, a Force Nine hit us, we ran out of water. I had others who'd been through it before so I just kind of just moulded into the groove. The new guys have got no one that's been out there for any extensive period of time. Their first big storm hits, they're low on supplies, and it's like: 'Oh my gosh, the end of the world'. I'm sure had it been David Lee Stone, Jessie Brandon, Tommy Rivers and myself it wouldn't have been.'

When asked about what would happen with the Americans who were on board Charlie answered: "Nothing at all. They haven't done anything wrong. From what I understand they're at immigration now, which is the normal procedure and I presume they will just be matter-of-factly released and on their way."

Anglia TV also brought a short chat with one of the British crew members, Captain Patrick Paternoster, who was asked what the morale was aboard the radio ship: "We're all happy. Happy go lucky. None of us have got bruises, black eyes or anything".

Captain Patrick 'Salty' Paternoster was also mentioned on November 8th in the Ipswich Evening Star: 'An Ipswich man has today emerged as a central figure in the Radio Laser drama. Captain Patrick 'Salty' Paternoster is among the six British crew members who have been interviewed by police and could be prosecuted. Today Captain Paternoster, of Holbrook Road, was thought to still be on board the vessel and his Ipswich family was awaiting news of him. Bachelor 'Salty', who shares a home with his brother Dennis, has been at sea since the age of 16.'

For those who thought the Communicator could go outside again to international waters within days the last straw went as on November the 8th Radio Orwell brought the sad news: 'There's been a fresh blow for the pirate radio station Laser. Its ship, the MV Communicator, has been declared unsafe by the Department of Trade and Industry.' Of course it's normal that ships coming into a harbour have a routine check by the authorities and in the case of the Communicator inspectors found mechanical faults, which made the ship unsafe. A ship labelled 'unsafe' can only leave a harbour if the authorities, in this case the Department of Trade and Industry, are satisfied that a ship is back in safe working order.

Some days later, when all on board had left without any charges being brought, Craig Novack told what the real problem was: "We had a problem with the generators on board; just about every generator went kaput all at the same time. It was basically a matter of bad luck that everything went all at once. We had some rough weeks out there, force ten winds and it was the opinion that it was not safe anymore to be out there in the condition that we were in, so it was the Captain's decision to bring the ship in. We had a round of bad luck with the equipment on board. You know, just everything packed up and decided not to work any longer. The engineer on board was unable to get it all going again and because of the weather that was out there, we needed certain generators to be sure that we can, if we have to, move away from sandbanks or something like that kind of thing. And we weren't in a safe position so the Captain decided that for our safety it was the best idea to bring it in.'

John Catlett had in an interview in Offshore Echos magazine in 1987 in which he outlined his own unique memories to the day the ship came into Harwich harbour: 'One of the most touching moments occurred at the very end when the ship came into Harwich. The disc jockeys were allowed to sleep onboard the vessel overnight so that they would come off and be processed by the immigration authorities the next morning, rather than bring the officials in at night when they weren't normally working."

"Having spoken to the staff that night when the ship came in, I went off and came back the next morning, went back out again on a police launch and accompanied the disc jockeys to the immigration officer who found some documents in various states of disarray. One had been admitted to the U.K. more than six months previous and his visa had run out. Another had arrived on the Communicator from Holland and had never been approved entry into the U.K. The authorities didn't know quite what to do so they interviewed each of the disc jockeys individually and we sat around and waited for a couple of hours."

"When the interviews were finished, we were all grouped in a room together. I was there as their 'protector' and I was promising that they wouldn't become 'wards of the State' and that I would make sure that they would have enough money to get home and so on. The officials said that as the disc jockeys were not likely to be threats to the Crown, they were going to give each of them a one-month visa and hope that they all would visit Britain and enjoy the country as tourists. They said that there would be no penalties if they would be willing to cooperate by giving their autographs! I thought that was very touching."

The Evening Star added that 'the vessel had been arrested by the Admiralty Marshall, a writ fixed to the mast and a 'keeper' put on board to prevent her leaving port. Marshall Vincent Ricks said it will remain impounded till the debts of 7,000 Pounds, owed by the company running the station, is paid. It is said to be owed by Paul

Rusling, of Hull, for installing radio transmitters and broadcast consultancy work. He took out the writ. Laser's manager Catlett has denied any knowledge of the debt.'

On November 15th in Broadcast, it was mentioned that the millionaire backer, Dublin based Smyth, was no longer prepared to invest further money. The same day Campaign mentioned that the new Laser's office in New York was closed and that the answering machine drawled: 'Laser 558 is off air because of a combination of circumstances, bad weather, bad luck and logistical problems, but certainly not because of a lack of listener or advertiser support. It was also mentioned that the future plans were indefinite at the time but they appreciated the interest and support. The US Trade paper 'Radio and Records' in its November 15th edition quoted John Catlett : "Our offices in New York have been flooded with phone calls and it would seem to us there are a lot of people who want us back."

On November 16th we had telephone contact again with Catlett who said that several repairs had been done and also the radar was at 100% in good condition again. He added that the ship was towed further up the river, behind a bridge, so no sudden departure would be made. A day later Catlett was interviewed on Dutch Radio VOO where he was asked about the debts the station would have with Paul Rusling. Catlett denied they had to pay Rusling. He also said that he would be leaving for America as soon as possible to find new investors to bring Laser 558 back. November 23rd we again took some time for phone-calls and learned that Charlie Wolf, as well as Tommy Rivers, flew back to the USA at their own expense.

Time to see what John Catlett had to answer to the question from Chris Edwards in August 1987: What were the basic problems with the operation? "In the final months, after we moved the New York office, we brought in more money and advertising than it cost us to operate the ship. But by that time, we had substantial debts that had been run up by Music Media International in New York. So, when the ship went off the air, I would say that thirty people were still owed money, myself included."

And when he was asked about the general feeling amongst the staff during the last few months of Laser 558, he answered: "Well, Euro siege made no sense to us because we couldn't understand why the British Government was spending so much money to do something that annoyed us but didn't interfere with our broadcasting. It gave us tremendously publicity. On the other hand, it did quite frankly, make some potential advertisers nervous about advertising with us. It didn't drive away any of the advertisers that we had. It just may have discouraged some potential advertisers."

"The problems in the end, when we had a captain, who either didn't receive or didn't follow orders, was a disaster. A captain who didn't have enough training to repair equipment that other captains, we had hired at other times, would have easily repaired. With another captain on board, we might not have come in and might be broadcasting today. The general feeling after coming in into Harwich harbour was that the captain had scuppered our opportunity to stay in business."

We mentioned that Laser 558 and Radio Caroline were accused of interfering on several channels. Johnny Lewis recalls an interesting evening on certain channels: "We talked a lot with those on the Communicator and one night Charlie Wolf and I just talking to each other. We always had people trying to break into our chats on CB; one night we upped the power and said: "Yah, come in on the side." Six and a half hours later, after the entire CB clubs of Essex, Suffolk and Kent had been talking to us, it was about five in the morning. I started to switch channels, when Charlie was still talking to those people. I thought that I just go and see what else is going on and there wasn't another channel on CB being used. Everybody was on the channel we were using. It was unbelievable!"

"We even had people from a lifeboat coming in. Somebody using the CB, not on the lifeboat but the guy worked on a lifeboat, told me that it was all absolutely crap, all this interference business and there has never been any interference reported. Then there was a chap driving home from RAF Manston and said they never had any problems either. We have had everybody calling us up on the RT, different ships, ferries and even warships, all saying: "Don't let those buggers beat you!" We have had loads of boats calling us up on the radio telephone just to pledge their support to us; the dredgers have all said they've never had any problems with us. In fact, most boats that sailed past us have actually complained more about some of the BBC broadcasts interfering with their equipment than us."

At the end of December 1985, the MV Communicator was anchored in the River Stour off Ewarton, where she could be easily seen from the North Bank. Captain Paternoster had left the ship and was replaced by a new captain. The rest of the crew remained on the ship and all the DJs had left. Some flew back to the USA, others wanted to find a job within the British media industry.

It took several months before I saw an official statement in the newspapers which could led to a radio future for Laser's former radio ship. In the Daily Express dated March 27th, 1986 I read that the good ship Communicator was for sale: 'It was five months ago that the ship's Jolly Roger, flying about 20 miles of the Essex coast, lost its smile in a force nine gale. The SOS went out and, with a blown generator spelling the end of illegal broadcasting, the ship was escorted into Harwich by the DTI and immediately arrested. But now, because of an official 'slip up' the ageing bulkheads could soon be all at sea again with her original owner.

Laser ended up in the Admiralty Court of the High Court, because creditors were demanding to be paid. The order went out: 'Sell the ship'. The Admiralty Marshal, Vincent Ricks, has confirmed that the Communicator will be sold with all her equipment intact.'

In an interview, Ricks mentioned that a lot of interest was shown and that the Communicator would be sold 'lock, stock and barrel.' The big question was, whether there was anything to stop some buccaneering spirit from buying the MV Communicator and sailing her out again, starting the transmitters and put a new station on the air, but that's another story. Laser 558 was history forever and would not come back on the air under that name. Laser 558 did change the radio industry in Britain dramatically and brought a faster format to most of the competitors and, most of all, ended the needle time restrictions on the British Radio Industry.

And for the DJ Jeff Davis, a rare event happened years later: "Three years after my return in the USA I began dating an attractive British woman who lived in Tucson. Since she was British, I asked her if she had heard of Laser 558. She had yes. When I told her I worked the 1 to 5pm shift her eyes lit up with disbelief. It turns out that as a nurse she had pulled her back lifting a patient. She was in traction for a period of time and listened to me on Laser! The lady specifically remembered the 'Happy Hour'; I did during the 4-5pm hour where I would invite other members of the crew to join me. I presented it with sound effects like we were in a pub doing a live broadcast. What a small world!"

For more information about Laser 558

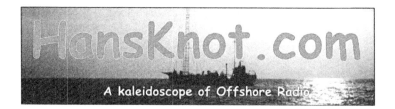

HansKnot.com

Laser books & other products:

WorldofRadio.co.uk/Laser.html

Offshoreradio.de

More books about Laser 558

There were 11 different stations broadcast from the Communicator. It's of the most action packed stories of offshore radio. A story of gangsters, crooks and fraudsters, of a Government blockade on supplies, the dramas, an armed raid, 'middle of the night" boardings, take-overs and more. The heroes are the gallant crew of DJs and brave bunch of engineers who kept the music and entertainment flowing against all odds while a few landlubbers coined in millions of pounds & guilders.

£19.95

Laser Radio programming is about the policy and techniques of major offshore stations, especially Radio Caroline, and Laser plus 'the big Daddy station whose style and fresh format that inspired the Laser founders, 66 boss station - SRE Swinging Radio England.

The programming book has details of all the voices heard on Laser, (730, 558 & Laser Hot Hits) a reprint of Laser's full Operations Manual and a discussion on the format, music playlisting, strap lines, trailer production and other techniques that Laser used to attract an audience of ten million.   **£15.95**

https://WorldofRadio.co.uk/Laser.html

181

Printed in Great Britain
by Amazon

77070474R00108